Everything You Wanted
to Know about Indians

Everything
You Wanted
to Know about
INDIANS
But Were Afraid to Ask

Anton Treuer

BOREALIS
BOOKS

10/2012

Borealis Books is an imprint of the Minnesota Historical Society Press.

www.mhspress.org

The Minnesota Historical Society Press is a member of the Association of American University Presses.

Manufactured in the United States of America

10 9 8 7 6 5 4 3 2

♾ The paper used in this publication meets the minimum requirements of the American National Standard for Information Sciences—Permanence for Printed Library Materials, ANSI Z39.48–1984.

International Standard Book Number
ISBN: 978-0-87351-861-1 (paper)
ISBN: 978-0-87351-862-8 (e-book)

Library of Congress Cataloging-in-Publication Data

Treuer, Anton.
    Everything you wanted to know about Indians but were afraid to ask
      / Anton Treuer.
    p. cm.
    Includes bibliographical references and index.
    ISBN 978-0-87351-861-1 (pbk. : alk. paper) — ISBN 978-0-87351-862-8 (ebook)
    1. Indians—History. 2. Indians—Social life and customs. 3. Indians in popular culture. I. Title.
    E77.T795 2012
    909'.0491411—dc23
                                                            2011053026

For Isaac,
with high hopes that the world
in which you raise your children will be
kinder and more understanding
than this one

Contents

Do they charge for participation in native ceremonies?

What is a sweat lodge?

Do Indians still get persecuted for their religious beliefs?

What is a powwow?

What do the different styles of dance mean?

Why are "49" songs sung in English?

How come they have a prize purse at powwows?

Can white people dance at powwows?

Do women sing at powwows?

What is the protocol for gifts at powwows?

How many tribal languages are spoken in North America?

Which ones have a chance to be here a hundred years from now?

Why are fluency rates higher in Canada?

It seems like tribal languages won't give native people a leg up in the modern world. Why are tribal languages important to Indians?

Why should tribal languages be important to everyone else?

What are the challenges to successfully revitalizing tribal languages?

When were tribal languages first written down?

Many tribal languages were never written. Why do they write them now?

Why is it funnier in Indian?

How do tribal languages encapsulate a different world view?

159 Conclusion: Finding Ways to Make a Difference
   How can I help?

Everything You Wanted
to Know about Indians

Introduction: Ambassador

> "Be who you are and say what you feel,
> because those who mind don't matter
> and those who matter don't mind."
>
> ATTRIBUTED TO DR. SEUSS

INDIANS. They are so often imagined, but so infrequently well understood.

I grew up in a borderland. My family moved a couple times, but we usually lived on or near the Leech Lake Reservation in northern Minnesota. I went to school in the nearby town of Bemidji with plenty of other native kids and many more whites. The town's racial composition has changed a lot since then, but in the 1970s and 1980s, it was all whites and Indians. Although the town is surrounded by the three largest reservations in Minnesota (in geographic size and population), the two worlds rarely interacted. The school took kids on field trips to Minneapolis, 225 miles away, rather than to the neighboring native communities. But Indians could be terrifying to members of the white community, and when presented with angry looks and few opportunities to safely learn about their neighbors and the first people of the land, they usually just stuck to their imaginings.

That borderland I grew up in was more than an awkward physical nexus of races and communities. It was a divided and confusing place politically, legally, intellectually, and culturally. The tribes maintained their own governments and rarely got in-

1

volved in the American political process, especially at the local level. And no outsider ever felt like he or she had any authority to ask about, much less comment on or participate in, anything happening on the rez. The web of contradictory jurisdictions and agencies that dealt with criminal affairs and Indian land never made much sense to anyone of any race.

Indians hadn't written many books, and school districts and the general public would never open up to Vine Deloria, Jr., and the few other "radical" Indians who had actually managed to get anything in print. Most of the elders on the rez had gone to government-run residential boarding schools. Their children (the parental generation of my youth) had developed a serious distrust of the government and educational institutions as a result. Educators and administrators resented the parents' absence at school conferences and the truancy issues for many native students, but nobody talked about the bigger issues, which sat like a giant bear in the corner of the room every time the schools and native families interacted. My family and every one of my uncles and aunts harvested wild rice, snared rabbits, and made maple syrup every year, but most of my nonnative peers did not.

Although I had several painful experiences with overt racial discrimination as a young person, I had some great friends in high school. I was truly inspired by my history teacher, Thomas Galarneault, whose lectures and support made a significant contribution to my lifelong interest in education and history. I had encouragement from Marlene Bergstrom in the guidance office. And I was a great student. But the borderland was a bramble on every level. I was tired of the tension, the confusion, and the mean-spirited statements of my peers about "drunken Indians." I applied to Princeton University on a whim and surprised everyone, from my peers to my parents and especially myself, when I got in. I had found a way out. Or I thought I had.

I was looking forward to a breath of fresh air and a respite from the borderland of my youth as much as I was to the challenges of a new stage of life. And those years remain some of my most treasured. But I still had a profoundly well-educated Princetonian ask me, "Where is your tomahawk?" Another time, a woman approached me in the college gymnasium and exclaimed, "You have the most beautiful red skin." I was too flabbergasted to respond. I took a friend to see *Dances with Wolves* and was told, "Your people have a beautiful culture." My people come from the Great Lakes rather than the Plains and from the modern age rather than the nineteenth century, but again I had no response. I made many lifelong friends at college, and they supported but also challenged me with questions like, "Why should Indians have reservations?"

By my junior year I realized I had not escaped the borderland. No matter how far I traveled, the haze engulfed everyone I met. Indians were imagined, not understood. And there was a dearth of resources and opportunities to do anything about it. I wanted to come home.

Homesick though I was, I was *not* going to be another statistic by dropping out of school. I toughed it out at college but started a quest to learn more about myself. I no longer wanted to run from the borderland: I wanted to understand it better and do something to make it easier for others to traverse.

While at Princeton, I heard that a Comanche medicine woman named Barrett Eagle Bear was coming to New Jersey from Texas to run sweat lodge ceremonies. Hungry for a taste of home, I drove out to the wooded area where she would conduct her ceremony and found, to my great surprise, over fifty naked white people standing in the woods, waiting. One man was holding a staff adorned with a pair of deer antlers and chicken feathers. With great trepidation, I opened the car door. I was immediately approached by a naked white woman, roughly sixty years of age and around 190 pounds. She folded me into a tight embrace, saying, "I am so sorry for what my people have done to your people."

Throughout my life, if I have ever thought or said that I had seen it all, I was soon shown something new. Part of me was furious at what looked like a bunch of white people playing Indian. This was not real. I started to question whether Eagle Bear was even Indian for allowing the charade. Part of me wanted to laugh, because anyone who got a hug like that from a naked elder really couldn't do anything else. But as I carefully separated myself from her embrace, I looked at her face. She was filled with genuine remorse, on the verge of tears. Respect was a value deeply embedded in my being from my upbringing and cultural experience. Lines on her face showed the wisdom of age and experience. I couldn't laugh. And I couldn't just yell at her or give her a mean look and drive away. And in a flash, my running from the borderlands and my desire to find a way for others to travel through them brought me an epiphany.

I was not just another Indian. No Indian really is. Because we are so often imagined and so infrequently understood, I was (both unfairly and rightly) an ambassador for my people. If the morass of misunderstandings that made growing up native so frustrating for me was ever to be remedied, I would have to do my part to shine some light on the brambles and try to clear a path for others. As that old woman looked up at me, I knew that I was probably the first Indian she had ever met and, though it wasn't fair to anyone, my reaction would be a testament to the character of my entire race. So I didn't laugh. I didn't rise to anger. I didn't call her out or drive away. I very politely said, "Could you put some clothes on? I would love to talk to you about all of this."

She put some clothes on. And we talked. I explained that for ceremonies at home we usually covered up in the presence of others, especially with men and women present. We discussed the ceremony, geography, custom, and practice. We talked about history. I explained my feeling that guilt for whites and anger for Indians were doing nothing to make the world a better place, especially for the people who harbored such emotions, understandable though they are. The secret was to turn anger and guilt into positive action.

That's how I learned a few things from an unexpected and unlikely source in the New Jersey woods. I learned something about the borderland. Communication requires a safe space for discourse, an opportunity for genuine connection, and authentic, reliable information. And I learned something about myself.

When I commit to something, I always go all the way. The decks on my house could withstand an earthquake measuring 6.0 on the Richter scale. I have nine children. I take my job as role model for my children and ambassador for my people seriously. I don't drink alcohol—not because I am a recovering addict (I have never inhaled anything, nor blacked out or vomited from drink) but because I want to send a message to my own people and to others. I want to redefine suppositions about what it means to be native. Abstaining is also important to the people whom I now serve at ceremonies: they are looking for a clean, sober place to heal, relying upon the integrity of the people who help at those ceremonies to provide that environment.

I gave up on my early plans of becoming an investment banker or lawyer. I never would have been happy in those roles. Instead, I graduated from Princeton with plans to walk the earth, which I did successfully for several months before I had to take a job. But I dedicated myself to the pursuit of my tribal language, culture, and history. I eventually went to graduate school and entered academia. Through it all, I maintained one foot in the wigwam and one in the ivory tower, but I still see the borderland every day out my bedroom window.

This book is designed as a tool to help all people navigate that space. Readers can read straight through, peruse the sections, or use the contents and index to find answers to specific questions. Above all, I want this work to provide a place for people to get answers. It offers a critical first step to comfortably dispel erroneous imaginings and develop deeper understandings.

I have now given hundreds of public lectures on a variety of subjects. This book first emerged as part of the question and answer sessions that followed my presentations. Within these safe spaces, people raised a torrent of questions. Although curricula is constantly under revision in public schools, we still have a long way to go to make it easy for native and nonnative peoples to learn about Indian history, culture, and current events. A good friend of mine, Michael Meuers, eventually suggested the title of this book as the headline for some of my public lectures. Since then, the appeal of this subject has grown dramatically, bringing me all over the United States and Canada to conduct teacher trainings and give public speeches.

Before launching into the substance of the questions and answers that form the guts of this book, I also want to make a major disclaimer. Just as no white person can speak for all white people, I cannot speak for all Indians. It would be unfair to ask, "What do all white people think about abortion?" Of course, there is a diversity of opinion on that subject and nearly every other important subject you may raise. It is the same for Indians. My experiences have taught me what questions people have about Indians, and I am motivated to pull those questions together here and address them. I write mostly about the Ojibwe, because that is what I know, and in many cases you will gain specific rather than generic answers. But I also provide examples and information about a few of the hundreds of other Indian nations that have populated this continent.

Some of the current issues I engage—including subjects of identity, tribal citizenship, casinos, mascots, and cultural revitalization—evoke strong and divergent responses from native people. I am candidly giving my opinions, and the difference between fact and opinion should be clear to you. But I cannot and do not claim to represent "the native view" in this book. My responses reflect only the view of one native person, and they have to be read with this understanding. Perhaps, given answers to the questions in this work, you will feel better able to seek out different opinions from other native people.

Thank you for taking the time to read this book. I sincerely hope that it will make a contribution to breaking down barriers and advancing understanding of Indians for all people.

Terminology

When asked what Indians called North America before Columbus arrived, noted scholar Vine Deloria, Jr., simply replied, "Ours."

What terms are most appropriate for talking about North America's first people?

The word *Indian* comes from a mistake: on his first voyage to the Americas, Columbus thought the Caribbean was the Indian Ocean and the people there were Indians. The use of the word and assumptions around it are well documented in Columbus's writings and those of other Spanish officials who accompanied him on the voyage and corresponded with him. Russell Means, Peter Matthiessen, George Carlin, and a few others have claimed that the word *Indian* is actually derived from the Spanish phrase *una gente in Dios* (people of God). But Columbus never used that phrase in reference to any people in the Americas.[1] Use of the word *Indian* had nothing to do with the words *in Dios*. It was a mislabeling based on Columbus's confusion about where he was when he first arrived in the Americas—and it stuck, even after the mistake was well known in Europe.

I use the word *Indian* in this book intentionally and with full knowledge of its shortcomings as a misnomer that gives some people offense. I have no fundamental opposition to what some label as "political correctness," and in making decisions about labels, I try to use ones that are respectful but also

7

clear. However, the terms *native, indigenous, First Nations person,* and *aboriginal* are often ambiguous, equally problematic, and in some cases more cumbersome. I also find Sherman Alexie's remark resonant: "The white man tried to take our land, our sovereignty, and our languages. And he gave us the word 'Indian.' Now he wants to take the word 'Indian' away from us too. Well, he can't have it."[2]

As much as possible, we should all use tribal terms of self-reference in writing about each tribe: they are authentic and loaded with empowered meaning. Those words (such as *Diné, Ho-Chunk, Dakota, Anishinaabe,* or *Ojibwe*) work at the level of tribal discussion, but they sound ethnocentric to members of other tribes. Regardless of all decisions about labels, however, it is most critically important that we respect one another and create an environment in which it is safe to ask any thoughtful question without fear. The only way to arrive at a deeper understanding is to make it acceptable to ask anything you wanted to know about Indians but were afraid to ask and get a meaningful answer rather than an angry admonition.

What terms are *not* appropriate for talking about North America's first people?

It's important that fear of sounding ignorant or racist does not paralyze communication about Indians. Knowing what terms to use can help ease that fear, but knowing what terms to avoid can be just as important. Most native people frown on use of the words *squaw, brave,* and *papoose.* These are words that create distance, use hurtful clichés to point out difference, and say clearly that "those people" are not like normal people.

Squaw is considered particularly offensive. The true origins of the word are a subject of some debate. Some Indian activists and even scholars have asserted that it is actually a corruption of a Mohawk word for female genitalia, although that theory has been largely debunked by linguist Ives Goddard and others.[3] Others assert that it is derived from the Cree word for woman, *iskwe,* or its Ojibwe variant, *ikwe.* Considering its first use by the French, the latter seems more likely. The words in Massachusett and other Algonquian languages on the Atlantic seaboard are quite similar to Cree and may be the more likely origin of the word's transfer to English. Regardless of origin, however, it has often been used as a negatively value-laden term, and most native people find it truly insulting. Most special terms for minority women have similar perceptions (Negress, Jewess). There is ongoing work to change many place names (Squaw Valley, Squaw Lake) into something less offensive, but those efforts are sometimes met with resistance.

What terms are most appropriate for talking about each tribe?

Each tribe has its own terms of self-reference. Finding the appropriate labels can be confusing because the tribal terms of self-reference are not necessarily those employed by the U.S. or Canadian governments. Sometimes they are not even the same as the terms used by tribal governments.

The Ojibwe are a perfect example of this. The word *Chippewa,* frequently used in reference to the Ojibwe, especially in the United States, is actually a corruption of *Ojibwe.* Europeans frequently missed subtleties of Ojibwe pronunciation, hardening sounds and omitting letters. The soft *j* was written down as *ch,* and the soft *b* was written as *p.* The *o* was not even written, and the *e* was written as a short *a.* There have been numerous alternative spellings. But the term *Chippewa* was incorporated into the bureaucratic mechanisms of the U.S. government and never changed. Even today, the Bureau of Indian Affairs (the agency that deals with Indians) uses *Chippewa.* Furthermore, the term was formally incorporated into the constitutions of all Ojibwe reservations in America because those documents were drafted by the U.S. government rather than by tribal people.

Tribal advocacy for the original term *Ojibwe* is slowly winning out now, however, as many reservations have officially incorporated it into their tribal names and constitutions, with several notable exceptions. Constitutional reform is cumbersome and contentious at any level of politics, and widely supported terminology change often gets sidelined by other more disputed issues like tribal enrollment. Ojibwe people today use the term *Ojibwe* as a tribally specific term for self-reference (Ojibwe only) but also use *Anishinaabe* to refer to all Indians—Ojibwe, Dakota, and others. The word *Anishinaabe* is used as commonly as *Ojibwe* by tribal members in everyday conversation, which has led to some confusion about their distinctions, but *Ojibwe* is tribally specific and *Anishinaabe* is inclusive of all tribes.

For most tribes, there is one tribal term of self-reference and one other term, either corrupted from the original or entirely foreign. Such is the case for the people the Spanish called *Navajo* but who call themselves *Diné*. Early European explorers named the tribal groups they saw, often ignoring the people's own names for themselves. This happened for the Ho-Chunk, whom the Ojibwe called *Wiinibiigoog,* meaning "people of the muddy water," which the French corrupted into *Winnebago.*

Dialect issues within a tribal group occasionally cause confusion as well. The word *Sioux,* derived from the Ojibwe term *Naadowesiwag* (a species of snake), was a code word for "enemy" and often frowned upon by Dakota tribal members. The people called *Sioux* are really comprised of three major language groupings—Dakota, Nakota, and Lakota—who formed an alliance known as the Oceti Sakowin (Seven Council Fires). The Lakota further diversified into seven more bands. But the Dakota are not the Lakota; calling them Oceti Sakowin still leaves outsiders unsure of which group is being discussed; and sometimes scholars and even tribal members use the term *Sioux* as an expedient way to speak about the entire grouping in spite of the issues with the term.

How do I know how to spell all these complicated terms?

In discussion of tribes, it is usually best to use the preferred spelling of their respective reservation tribal governments (*Potawatomi, Menominee, Ottawa, Assiniboine,* and *Ho-Chunk,* for example).[4] Sometimes tribal government spellings do not reflect the preferred spellings of tribal members or accepted orthographies, but they are your safest bet.

What term is most appropriate—*nation, band, tribe,* or *reservation*?

Prior to the first European efforts to colonize Indians, none of these labels were used by Indians to describe themselves, and the peoples of the two continents saw the concepts very differently. There was diversity in North America. The Aztec Empire had massive cities and ten million citizens. Their society was highly structured and perhaps the closest thing to what Europeans recognized as a nation. But the majority of tribes were smaller and simply called themselves "the people." In most of the Americas they lived in villages, and the village was the primary social and political unit in their lives. Even populous tribes like the Ojibwe, who occupied millions of acres of territory, did not function as a single political entity. Villages were autonomous. Today there are around two hundred Ojibwe villages (about two-thirds of them in Canada and one-third in the United States), but there were even more during the treaty period. And the Ojibwe were one of five hundred Indian tribes in North America.

Colonial powers, especially the British and Americans, wanted to simplify the politics so they could get at Indian land faster. That process started with the construction of new labels for native communities that in turn helped the evolution of new Indian political structures. So instead of making hundreds of treaties with each and every Ojibwe village, the U.S. government summoned numerous chiefs from many villages in a given area to a treaty conference and called them the chiefs of a certain *band*. The concept of band was as new as the label to the Ojibwe, but once the political process began, the label and the concept stuck.

Even today, the tribal citizenship cards of most Ojibwe people in Minnesota note the band with which they are affiliated—Mississippi, Pillager, Lake Superior, or Pembina, for example. Tribal governments also had the term *band* incorporated into their constitutions, which were created by the U.S. government, so those political labels permeate the legalese of tribal government today. And often there are two to four bands represented on each reservation. The concept of band meant a lot at treaty time, and it sometimes plays heavily in land claims cases today, but the label and concept mean little else to Ojibwe people. Many other villages were grouped together under common bands at treaty time when that concept and label did not previously exist. The term is not offensive, but it can be confusing.

The word *reservation* was applied to the lands that were reserved or set aside for various groups of Indians at treaty time. A reservation is the place that many native people call home, and even those who live elsewhere associate strongly with their home reservations. These are the places where most cultural and community events are held and where tribes spend their resources trying to strengthen their communities and prepare for the future.

The word *tribe* gets used two ways: as a label for all people of the same shared cultural group (as for the Ojibwe in their two hundred distinct communities) and also as a label for each reservation's government. Tribes, or tribal governments, are not just cultural enclaves. They are political entities, and complex laws impact and define the scope of their power. Tribes have power that supersedes that of state governments in many ways, making it possible for tribes to operate casinos, for example, without regard for state laws. A detailed explanation of tribal government, sovereignty, and law follows throughout this book, but the labels only make sense when one understands the concepts that inform them.

Tribes are in fact *nations*. They make laws, hold elections, administer funds, and interact with other governments. Because tribes are nations, tribal leaders and citizens often emphasize and reinforce their status by use of the word *nation*, and that term is preferred by some tribal people. The words *nation, band, tribe*, and *reservation* are sometimes used interchangeably, and none cause offense, but they all speak to the complicated history and evolving political landscape in Indian country.

What does the word *powwow* mean?

A Google search will reveal two full pages of definitions and conflicting answers to the linguistic origins of the word. The first usage of the term in English occurred in 1624. Most scholars agree that it is derived from a word in the languages of eastern Algonquian tribes (usually Narragansett or Massachusett) for spiritual leader. It was later misapplied to many types of ceremonial and secular events that involved dancing, and it has been spelled several different ways. See pages 68 to 78 for a substantive discussion of the history and cultural form of powwows today.

How can I find out the meaning of the place names around me that come from indigenous languages?

All languages are composed of roots, and those roots are loaded with meaning. In English, most roots come from the language's Latin, Greek, Celtic, and Germanic underpinnings, usually unknown to everyday speakers of English. But for most first speakers of tribal languages, the roots of words and their deeper meanings are often known.

For example, the city of Bemidji, Minnesota, derives its name from an Ojibwe word, *Bemijigamaag*, meaning "the place where the current cuts across," or "a river runs through it." That word describes the unique geographical configuration of the place. Four major watersheds converge and form a continental divide in Bemidji. The Red River watershed flows west and north toward Winnipeg. The Rainy River watershed flows north through the Big Fork River into Rainy River. The Lake Superior watershed flows east. And the Mississippi watershed begins by flowing northwest, pulled toward the Red River watershed, and then north, toward the Rainy River watershed. It then flows east, toward the Lake Superior watershed, before charting its own course southward to the Gulf of Mexico. Bemidji is located on the northernmost point of the Mississippi River. Prior to construction of the power dam on the Mississippi, Lake Bemidji was actually two separate lakes, connected by a shallow stretch of water off of Diamond Point. The Mississippi River did not flow through those two lakes; it simply cut across the corner of the largest one—a very uncommon geographical situation. But the indigenous population that lived in Bemidji had a deep understanding of its geography, of the watersheds pulling at the water from that place, and that understanding is reflected in the name they chose.

Most indigenous place names have similar deep meanings. It was very uncommon for a lake or village to be named after a person or another place, as in European naming and mapping conventions. When Europeans developed maps of the Americas, they often tried to use indigenous names for various locales. However, the complexity of the terminology led to many distortions in the record. To find the deeper meaning of the Indian names for the places in which you live, it is often necessary to do a little research. Fortunately, some great books, like Virgil Vogel's *Indian Names in Michigan* and Warren Upham's *Minnesota Place Names,* have done a lot of groundwork to help you understand places in the Great Lakes region. Also, the writings of early explorers such as Henry Schoolcraft and Frederic Baraga contain a wealth of information. There are similar books for other parts of the country—ask your local librarian for advice.

History

"The settlement of the North American
continent is just as little the consequence
of any claim of right in any democratic
or international sense; it was the consequence of a consciousness of right, which
was rooted solely in the conviction of the
superiority and therefore the right of
the white race."

ADOLF HITLER, Speech to the Industrie-
Klub of Düsseldorf (January 27, 1932)

How many Indians were in North and South America before contact?

The shortest and most honest answer to this question is that nobody knows for sure. Genomic and archaeological research is starting to give us more accurate information about how many groupings of people there were and the size of the communities and cities in which they lived. But a deep understanding of the true size of the indigenous population of the Americas at the time of Christopher Columbus is complicated.

Europeans brought diseases to which Indians had little natural immunity, and those diseases, traveling far faster than Europeans, rapidly depleted the native population. By the time Europeans were trying to explore the continental United States, the diseases they had brought to the coast had already ravaged the local settlements. Bartolomé de las Casas estimated that the indigenous population of Española, now known as Hispaniola, island of Haiti and the Dominican Republic, was two million people. Other Spanish chroniclers during Columbus's first four trips affirm that estimate—all for just one island in the Caribbean. The Spanish also estimated that the indigenous population within the Aztec Empire was more than ten million people. Archaeological evidence confirms that the capital city of the Aztec Empire was three times larger than the largest city in all of Western Europe at the time. Las Casas believed that the Spanish Empire killed between forty and fifty million people in Mesoamerica alone.

The East and West coasts of North and South America were very densely populated, more so than Western Europe. People in desert regions and the Great Plains spread out and competed more intensely for control of land and resources. Conservative estimates of the indigenous population of the Americas range from twenty to fifty million people. Others put the figure between seventy and ninety million or even more. Plenty of conflicting research and writing on the subject exist. A good way to get a handle on the various lines of thinking, to understand the work of prominent scholars, and to arrive at a reasonable conclusion is to read Charles Mann's book *1491: New Revelations of the Americas before Columbus.*

I find the higher estimates more convincing, but archaeologists have only scratched at about 1 percent of the earth's surface. Europeans chose many of the same sites as did Indians for their major settlements (Green Bay, St. Paul, Chicago, Milwaukee, New York, Mexico City), making archaeological research in these places more difficult. But archaeological research and new technologies continue to develop, and we will have more and better answers to this question in years to come.

When did Indians really get to North America?

Between 45,000 and 11,000 years ago, the buildup of continental ice sheets lowered sea levels and exposed a shelf of land between Alaska and Siberia.[1] Most archaeologists used to believe this was the primary route people took to enter the Americas, and some still do. But the dates and means by which the Americas were populated is a subject of much contemporary scientific debate.

Many American history books assert that Indians became the first Native Americans when they arrived in this hemisphere nine to ten thousand years ago by crossing this land bridge and moving down an "ice-free corridor" into the modern-day United States. Those books point to an archaeological site in Clovis, New Mexico, containing human-made tools used to kill large mammals as the oldest indisputable evidence of humans in the hemisphere.

This theory of human origin in the Americas (usually called the Clovis First Theory) is now widely challenged in the scientific community. Recent research on the Clovis site by Michael Waters, Thomas Stafford, and others has confirmed human evidence there between 10,900 and 11,050 years ago. At Monte Verde in Chile, Mario Pino and Thomas Dillehay found human tool marks on mastodon bones and evidence of human-made structures dating back 13,800 to 14,800 years. At the Meadowcroft Rockshelter in Pennsylvania, James M. Adovasio and other archaeologists have found tools, ceramics, lamellar blades, and lanceolate projectiles that are radiocarbon-dated 16,000 to 19,000 years old.

At least fifty other major archaeological sites also suggest evidence of human existence in the Americas anywhere from 19,000 to 50,000 years ago. Some sites show evidence of human beings in the Americas *before* the last land bridge connected the continents. Archaeologists are still arguing about the dates and the validity of many sites, but increasingly the scientific community is saying that the Clovis First model of human migration to the Americas is simply wrong. Most scientists now favor the theory that people came to the Americas either by land or by traveling along the Pacific Coast in boats long before the Clovis dates.

Why does it matter when Indians got here?

What those books do not always say, but do imply, is that "we are all immigrants here." That implication, no matter how inadvertent, has sometimes been used to defend or justify the dispossession and genocide of this land's first inhabitants. It is also important to note that when it comes to ancient civilizations (Egypt, Phoenicia, Greece, China), the earliest records we have are typically four to five thousand years old. There weren't even human beings anywhere in the British Isles twelve thousand years ago (the entire area was covered with ice). But there were Indians in the Americas then. No matter how one interprets the data, Native Americans are not immigrants. They are indigenous to the Americas.

What do Indians say about their origins?

There are Dakota people who know that Indians came from Spirit Lake. There are Hopi people who know that Indians emerged from the center of the earth in Arizona. There are Christians who know that the story printed in the Bible is an accurate description of humankind's arrival in the world. Some of those Christians are Indian, including a Pueblo man who told me that Jesus Christ traveled North America two thousand years ago; he was just known by a different name in Pueblo country. It is important to realize how divergent some of the origin beliefs held by native people are, and it is also critical to know that the people who hold these beliefs, like all other people of faith, are firmly convinced of their truth—and they are as deserving of respect.

Although there are significant differences among the origin beliefs of different tribes, there are some commonalities, too. All North American tribal origin stories describe a spiritual creation of humans. Most detail the physical place where humans were put on earth by the Great Spirit, and that place is in North America, albeit different parts of the continent depending on which tribal tradition is being consulted.

Many people deny scientific assertions about evolution in favor of religious explanations. But in addition to the religion/science debate, Indians often resist the dismissal of their understandings of origin, which disregards not only their knowledge but also their wisdom-keepers, elders, spiritual leaders, and very ways of knowing.

Who else made it here before Columbus?

Seafaring Polynesians definitely made it to South America. The sweet potato, indigenous to the Americas, proliferated throughout Polynesia prior to Columbus's trips to the Caribbean. Words from South American tribal languages traveled to Polynesia, and Polynesian peoples shared styles of watercraft with Indians in Chile. The Vikings also made it to maritime provinces in Canada about five hundred years before Columbus arrived in North America. Archaeological excavation offers evidence of their visits.

Did Native Americans scalp?

Yes. There has been some speculation that Europeans introduced scalping in North America as a form of bounty hunting. The lack of archaeological evidence of scalping prior to contact with Europeans suggests that it may not have happened in the Americas before their arrival. However, many historians do not accept this theory. If scalping originated in Europe, why was it primarily practiced in North America? Also, early seventeenth-century documents clearly show that scalping was an embedded custom when the French first entered the Great Lakes. Samuel de Champlain, for example, reported meeting the Algonquians at Tadoussac in 1603 when they were celebrating a victory over the Iroquois and dancing with about a hundred scalps. Many have argued that Europeans seized upon an older indigenous custom and transformed it into a bounty system during the French and Indian War and other conflicts as a

Scalp Dance, illustration by George Catlin, ca. 1844

way to encourage Indians to kill one another and to offer proof before being paid. Scalping was an entrenched native custom throughout the seventeenth, eighteenth, and early nineteenth centuries.[2]

Did Indians practice polygamy? Do they now?

Polygamy was a common practice among many tribes, a custom born of necessity. Men went off to war, traveled under dangerous conditions, went fishing on thin ice, and generally had much higher mortality rates than did women. Women had an immense work burden: raising crops, gathering and preserving foods, tanning hides, making clothing, and caring for small children. As a result, in many tribes men could have multiple wives, but women could have only one husband.

Although Native American polygamy evolved because of work and death dynamics rather than sexual power, the concept became culturally ingrained and the practice persisted long after the need for it had disappeared. It was more common for a man to marry two or three sisters rather than women from different families.[3] Some leaders, like Ojibwe chief Hole in the Day, used marriage as a way to advance political aspirations, but this was the exception rather than the rule. When mortality rates shifted and missionaries began to gain traction in many tribal communities, the practice of polygamy was abandoned by most tribes. A few tribes in South America still practice polygamy. Observing the dating habits of native teenagers, some North American tribal elders joke that select young people didn't get the message that the practice has ended.

What are native views about homosexuality?

Native American views on homosexuality are as varied and intense as those of the general population. Homophobia is just as rampant a problem in Indian country as it is anywhere else today. But the record shows that there was a respected and empowered place for homosexuals in historical Indian communities. The writings of George Catlin and *Jesuit Relations* are loaded with references to the respected and even exalted position held by homosexuals.

Gender identity can be very nuanced and complicated. But in many Indian communities, the most common variations of homosexuality were men who functioned as women in the traditional gendered division of labor and had male sexual partners, and women who functioned as men in all realms of the accepted gender role. The divisions of labor and social duty along gender lines usually left two primary groupings—male and female. A man who functioned as a woman in society usually adopted the customary clothing of women and performed the same duties and work as women. The same was true for women who wore the customary clothing and accepted the work and war duties traditionally reserved for men.

Today, the political and social fabric of Indian communities has changed dramatically. Gender is no longer a determining

George Catlin drew this rendition of a dance honoring a homosexual man while visiting the Sac and Fox Indians in the 1830s.

factor in political position for most tribes. Ceremonial life is the only realm that retains consistent vestigial reminders of the gendered division of labor. And in that realm there are still accepted transgender roles for homosexuals. Despite this history, mainstream media and social views probably have a greater impact on the perspectives of young native people today than the traditional values around gender roles or homosexuality. It is true that many Native Americans have a greater sensitivity to differential treatment based on race and gender and that Native Americans tend to vote for more Democrats than Republicans, which may indicate a somewhat more liberal modern political viewpoint among many, but certainly not all, native people.

How was gender configured in native communities?

Each tribe had its own culture and customs around gender, and the degree of variance between customs was significant. For social, political, and ceremonial functions, many tribes had a very strictly gendered division of labor.[4] Women and men each had specific duties and rights. They even wore different types of snowshoes.

Indian thinking about gender developed in ways dissimilar to European gender dynamics, where different duties often meant differential and unfair treatment of women. When asked why men and women sat on different sides of a ceremonial lodge, Mary Roberts, an elderly Ojibwe woman, explained that it was "to remind us that women and men each own half the lodge."[5] Usually, indigenous gender roles hinged on balance rather than equality. Often native women owned the home and had much greater power in marriage and divorce than did women in European societies. But not all tribal constructions of gender were beyond reproach. No culture should be romanticized or denigrated: like all others, Indians should be understood and evaluated on their own terms.

Do indigenous people in Canada get treated more fairly by their government than those in the United States?

Canadian Indians have not fared much better than their American relatives. Political and social developments for the indigenous populations of both countries have been parallel though not the same. The U.S. and Canadian governments both have attempted to undermine and diminish the status of tribal communities as sovereign nations. Both governments have actively participated in widespread efforts to assimilate the indigenous population. Native populations faced removal to reservations and had their children taken and sent to boarding schools. Widespread issues of substance abuse and an educational achievement gap plague native communities on both sides of the border.[6]

There are some differences. Canada is part of the British commonwealth of nations, and its independence was obtained through peaceful means rather than military revolution. For Canadian aboriginal people, this meant suffering through the colonial regimes of the French and British. Indigenous people in the United States had to suffer through—depending on the place—the colonial regimes of the Russian, Spanish, Dutch, French, British, and most importantly American governments. There were many ugly chapters in each of those colonial regimes, but some of the most intense physical violence was directed by the U.S. government and also state and local militias in the early American frontier age—the famous massacres often portrayed in movies.

Furthermore, the U.S. population is much larger than that of Canada, and 80 percent of Canadians live within fifty miles of the U.S. border. As a result, there are many parts of Canada where the indigenous population was and still is a majority. And many aboriginal communities in Canada are isolated, requiring a plane or boat for access. This relative degree of isolation has enabled some of these communities to maintain higher rates of fluency in their tribal languages and to rely more upon traditional lifeways such as hunting, fishing, and trapping to sustain themselves.

The British and Canadian governments have also differed from the United States in their legal configuration of tribal sovereignty. In the United States, the status of tribes as independent nations is verified and affirmed in treaty relationships and many court cases, leaving American Indians with a legally recognized and retained sovereignty. Canadian Indians have struggled to have their status as sovereign nations viewed as such or declared legally in provincial or federal courts. Ongoing efforts to affirm the sovereignty of First Nations in Canada have largely focused on political process and constitutional reform, creating another significant difference between the statuses of tribes in both countries.

It is not the case that Canadian Indians have fared better. There are differences in the two histories. The most essential features that define Indians as distinct groups of people and unique communities or nations—language, cultural practice, and belief—are threatened in both places. Many tribes, such as the Blackfeet and Ojibwe, have tribal communities on both sides of the border. Common geography, unifying cultural movements such as the powwow, and similar struggles serve to unify indigenous people in both places despite the differences in their histories.

What is the real story of Columbus?

The story of Christopher Columbus is one of the best known in our collective history but also one of the most misunderstood and misrepresented in our history books. I will try to separate fact from fiction and provide a different perspective on this deservedly famous figure in history.

In order to discuss the importance of Columbus in Indian history, we first have to lay out some of the background information in European history. In 1492, Spain had a long-standing trade feud with Portugal, and Portugal was winning. In 1486, the Portuguese Bartolomeu Diaz had rounded the Cape of Good Hope. Previously, the only way any European dared travel to India or China was through the Mediterranean and Middle East. In the Mediterranean were numerous pirates and middlemen whose activities raised prices on trade goods. Once Portuguese traders figured out how to get to Asia by going around the southern end of Africa, they could bring their goods to market at far less expense.

As was customary, the first European country to embark on a certain trade route or arrive in a certain "primitive" place claimed possession of that place, that route, and all human inhabitants of the "new" lands. The Portuguese laid claim to traveling around the south end of Africa. By 1498, now several years after Columbus's first trip to the Americas, Vasco da Gama made it all the way to India via Africa, and the route was exclusively Portuguese. At this time, France and England's navies were both quite weak compared to those of Spain and Portugal.

Spain was also running out of money, the result of staging an inquisition from 1480 to 1492. The depleted Spanish treasury had a big impact on Columbus and on Indians. In addition, Spain had been busy conquering Muslim towns in southern Spain. Much of Spain had been colonized by powerful nations from northern Africa between 711 and 718. However, by 1492, Spain had finally vanquished its foes and united the Iberian Peninsula. Columbus was funded by the Spanish monarchy not because they believed in him or his mission so much as because the small investment they made was worth the risk just in case Columbus was successful.

Christopher Columbus, as he is known by the Latin spelling of his name, was actually born Cristoforo Columbo, the son of a middle-class Genoese weaver, and became one of the most important figures in modern history. Although it is widely believed that Columbus was a genius for figuring out that the world was round, this information was common knowledge for all educated Europeans of the day. Sophisticated understanding of latitude had been developed by Eratosthenes in the year 300 BC. Eratosthenes also made the first estimate of the circumference of the globe and was accurate to within 2 percent of the correct measure. Sophisticated knowledge of longitude was developed by Ptolemy in the year AD 280. By the year AD 1000, most educated Europeans knew the earth was a sphere.

When Columbus beseeched the Spanish monarchy to fund his voyage, he did so with a boldness that surprises us still today. Even though Columbus was born a common man from Italy, he asked to become a Spanish noble. He also ambitiously requested one-tenth of the gold that was brought back on any trade route he might discover for the Spanish. Amazingly, both of those requests were granted.

He was also very lucky. The Portuguese and the Spanish staged voyages from different locations. If Columbus had sailed for any country other than Spain, he would probably not have been successful. Spain began most of its exploratory expeditions in the Atlantic from the Canary Islands. This launching point enabled Columbus to avoid the westerly trade winds and make it to the Americas. And, while sailors were uncomfortable sailing without the sight of land for many days, there was not a near mutiny on Columbus's first voyage.

Upon arriving in the Americas, Columbus made many important and interesting observations. All of his original journals, notes, and correspondence survive today in various archives throughout the world. We know a lot about what Columbus said, thought, and wrote. In his first letter to the Spanish monarchs after arriving in the "new world," he wrote, "Should your Majesty command it all the inhabitants could be taken away to Castile, or made slaves of on the island. With 50 men we could subjugate them all and make them do whatever we want."[7]

Columbus first arrived in the Bahamas. He then traveled to Española, what the Spanish called the present-day island of Haiti and the Dominican Republic, where he spent most of his time during his first voyage. The Spanish estimated the indigenous population of Española to be around two million people. Tribal people there accepted the Spanish as visitors and friends. Communication without a mutually intelligible language must have been extremely difficult, and there were many misunderstandings, including an exchange between Columbus and the principal Taino chief, Guacanagari. Columbus gave the chief a red cape and the chief gave him a tiara. The chief saw this as a fair exchange to cement a friendly trade relationship, but Columbus interpreted the gesture as one of submission—that the chief was surrendering his kingdom to Spanish authorities.

One of Columbus's three ships was damaged and had to be scuttled. As a result, when Columbus made preparations to return to Europe, he had to leave thirty-nine sailors behind. He brought with him small gold trinkets, food, and a few Indians. The Indians were captured in secret—they did not come willingly.

Upon returning to Spain, Columbus was received with incredible fanfare. He was granted all the primary requests made prior to his voyage. Columbus did not acquire large quantities of gold in the Americas. In fact, most of the gold he collected the Taino (Arawak) Indians had traded for with tribes from mainland Mexico. However, Columbus was sure to point out that there were vast quantities of gold to be had at Española. Columbus also asserted the availability of large quantities of resin, spices, and other valuable trade goods.

On Columbus's second voyage to North America, Spain sent a military force, numerous scribes, and many other officials and subordinates. The Spanish were surprised when they arrived at Española. The thirty-nine sailors left behind had all been killed. From their writings it soon became clear what happened. Lacking food, provisions, or means of subsistence, they survived by the good graces of their Indian hosts. The Spaniards became increasingly belligerent and took numerous Indians as slaves, using them to obtain food, to provide shelter, and for purposes of sexual gratification. Eventually, the Indian hosts grew tired of their maltreatment by the small number of Spaniards on their island. Remember, there were over two million Indian inhabitants and only thirty-nine Spaniards. Unrelenting, the Spaniards were eventually killed by the Indians. The returning Spanish force, however, saw this history as one of unprovoked Indian aggression. An assault on Spanish men was an assault on the Spanish king: the Indians had to be punished.

The Spanish government at Española immediately instituted a new policy. All Indians were required to bring one hawk's bell—about a quarter teaspoon—of gold dust to the Spanish four times every year. Chiefs were required to bring ten times that amount. This demand could not be met, however, because there were no large, readily available supplies of gold on Española. Most of the gold items in the Indians' possession were obtained from other tribes in trade from the Mexican mainland. Very soon the available gold supplies at Española were exhausted. For failing to meet the gold dust tribute, Indians had their hands chopped off by Spanish authorities—literally tens of thousands of Indians were killed this way. The Spanish immediately sent their army into the field to round up renegades and punish those who attempted to escape Spanish authority. The cruelties inflicted upon native people were so severe that many committed suicide by drinking cassava poison rather than submit to maltreatment at the hands of the Spanish.

Bartolomé de las Casas, a Jesuit priest and later bishop in the Catholic Church, accompanied Columbus on his second voyage and wrote several books about his observations in the "new world." In one of those books he wrote, "The Spanish are treating the Indians not as beasts, for beasts are treated properly at times, but like the excrement in a public square . . . Columbus was at the beginning of the ill usage inflicted upon them."[8] Las Casas went on to write,

> The Spaniards made bets as to who would split a man in two, or cut off his head at one blow; or they opened up his bowels. They tore babies from their mother's breast by their feet and dashed their heads against the rocks. They speared the bodies of other babes, together with their mothers and all who were before them, on their swords . . . They hanged Indians, and by thirteens, in honor and reverence for our Redeemer and the 12 apostles, and, with fire, they burned the Indians alive . . . I saw all the above things . . . All these did my own eyes witness.[9]

Why does getting the Columbus story right matter?

I have always been amazed that we know so much about Columbus but say so little about the dark side of his story. Columbus kept copious notes and numerous journals. Las Casas wrote several books on the subject. Those books were based on his firsthand observations of what happened during Columbus's voyages to the Americas. In spite of all we know, the version of events that we often teach our children is markedly different from what actually happened. This is starting to change: there are more and more revisions to ongoing curriculum and better resources available to those who teach it. However, we still have a long way to go to remedy the divergence between fact and mythology around Columbus. We have a long way to go in education. And we have an even longer way to go in educating our

This image is from a curriculum developed by Lifetime Learning Systems, Inc., and employed in the Milwaukee Public Schools system in the 1990s.

This drawing was rendered by Theodore de Bry (1528–98) to accompany the English printing of las Casas's work *In Defense of the Indians.*

society and changing our politics around the subject. Columbus is seen by most as a hero. There are more places named after Christopher Columbus in the United States of America than anyone else in history except for George Washington. And no wonder he is mythologized as a hero, given what we are teaching our children.

Grade school curricula often shows an Indian welcoming Columbus and Columbus ready to hug the Indian, with the caption, "In 1492, Columbus sailed the ocean blue." And frequently the words *celebrate* and *new world* are emphasized in this narrative. How can you discover a place when there are already people there? Obviously, Columbus did not discover America. It was a new world to Spaniards, but it was not a new world to Indians. It's now also clear that Polynesian people and Vikings also made it here long before Columbus.

But let's be fair. Columbus's mission established sustained permanent contact and communication between the Americas and the rest of the world. Neither the Vikings nor the Polynesians accomplished that. It was the culture of Spain and the rest of Europe during that time to make claims of discovery and possession. Columbus was, after all, a man of his times.

But consider this line of thinking. As I traveled in Europe some years ago, I wanted to see concentration camps. Outside the town of Munich, Germany, I looked for Dachau. However, there were no road signs until I was only one kilometer away. It seemed like the Germans were hiding that camp, like they were ashamed of it. I then went to Austria, and I looked for Mauthausen concentration camp. I found it, but there, too, I only found road signs about two kilometers away. Austria had joined Germany with the Anschluss and had culpability in the Final Solution—they had something to be ashamed of, too. But if you go to Auschwitz in Poland, you will see signs 200 kilometers away, 150 kilometers away, 100 kilometers away, 50, 25, 10. You can't miss it. It's like they were saying, "Look what the Nazis did to us."

All human beings have dark chapters in their personal histories. And all nations have dark chapters in their histories. Guilt is not a positive emotion. And looking at this history is not intended to make anyone feel guilty. However, it is important for all countries and all individuals to examine dark chapters in order to learn from them and prevent them from reoccurring. The Germans had to mandate instruction about the Holocaust in grades K–12. They had to make formal apologies for the culpability of the German people in the Nazis' Final Solution. And the German government had to make reparations to Holocaust survivors. These steps and actions in no way made up for everything that happened during the Holocaust. However, they did make it possible to have a conversation about healing and to help mitigate the chance of a holocaust ever happening again in Germany.

Here in the United States, very little effort has been made to voice formal apologies, make reparations, or pass political mandates about education.[10] Yet this country was founded in part by genocidal policies directed at Native Americans and the enslavement of black people. Both of those things are morally repugnant. Still, I love my country. In fact, it is because I love my country that I want to make sure that the mistakes of our past, our dark chapters, do not get repeated. We cannot afford to sugarcoat the dark chapters of our history, as we have for decades upon decades. It is time for that to stop.

In 1992, on the 500th anniversary of Columbus's first voyage, we had an opportunity to set the record straight and to strive for healing. We know a lot about Columbus. The stories were not hiding; people were hiding the stories. But in 1992, instead of saying, "Let's make the next 500 years different," the U.S. government simply established the Quincentenary Jubilee Commission. It is hard for many people to see how much damage is done by pretending there were no ugly chapters in American history.

Then-president George Bush, Sr., received a first-class education in the United States. However, no American president has written his own speeches since Abraham Lincoln. Each has a staff of smart and educated people with a huge amount of resources to craft policy and speech. Bush and his staff could have done so much better. Some of the words that jumped out at me from his statement on Columbus include *greatest achievements, discovery, milestone, great navigator, determination, Christopher Columbus Quincentenary Jubilee Commission, commemoration, opened the door to a new world, set an example for us all.* Yes, his example was followed, but it is not one I would like my children to emulate.

Like Christopher Columbus, George Bush, Sr., was a man of his times. However, it is important that we do not give our leaders a pass. We have enough information and resources to get this story right. We do not have to sugarcoat our history. On the contrary, we owe it to those who died and suffered to tell the truth, and we owe it to future generations not to lie to them. When teaching high schoolers, it is easy to look at the writings of someone like las Casas and talk about different perspectives on Columbus. At many schools, Columbus is put on trial and students argue both cases—that he was a man of his times and needs to be understood as such, and that his actions were unforgivable. No matter the conclusions, this activity certainly provides a more well-rounded discussion and understanding of Columbus.

I am also well aware that teaching grade schoolers is a different matter. However, there is still no need to glorify what for many people is a day of mourning. Native Americans changed the world with the introduction of many different types of food, medicine, obsidian scalpels still used in modern surgery today—all kinds of things—and the rest of the world changed Indians, and some of those changes were positive. Examining these gifts is a better entry point for discussion of this part of the historical narrative than glorifying the beginning of a colonial regime that killed millions. And make no mistake about it—there is glorification of this conquest.

Depicted on the great seal for the Territory of Wisconsin is an image of an Indian facing west, apparently boarding a steamship. The natives of that state, the Ho-Chunk, or Winnebago, were subjected to nine separate removal orders. Some were forcibly relocated from the region by being boarded onto steamships and sent to Santee, Nebraska. On the seal is also a white farmer industriously plowing up the land, plus the emergence of the state capitol building in the background. And the Latin caption says it all: "Civilization Succeeds Barbarism." There is no way to interpret this seal other than as a glorification of the forcible removal of Indian people from Wisconsin and the land being turned over to whites.[11] We sugarcoat our history, which enables us to celebrate even the ugliest chapters. We need to think real hard about why we do that and what message it sends to our children.

The great seal of the Territory of Wisconsin

There are some great resources available for teachers. *Rethinking Columbus,* by Rethinking Schools, is a practical guide for developing a curriculum. Whether you are teaching kindergartners or high schoolers, there is something here for you. Units about the Columbian Exchange—the transfer of ideas, technologies, and raw materials between Indians and the rest of the world—are a great entry point for younger kids. Appropriate for middle schoolers or high schoolers are more substantive discussions of Columbus and the resource material for teaching about him. I also recommend *Columbus: His Enterprise* by Hans Koning, which synthesizes much of the available research and writing on Columbus in an easy, user-friendly format.

What is the real story of Thanksgiving?

There are parts of the Wampanoag-Puritan relationship that have been correctly incorporated into the Thanksgiving narrative. But there are many dimensions to Puritan-Indian relations that have been greatly embellished and exaggerated.

Chief Massasoit of the Wampanoag forged a peaceful relationship with the Puritans. A Patuxet Indian named Tisquantum, or Squanto, who had briefly been a captive in England, lived with the Wampanoag in the early 1600s when this relationship developed. Massasoit, Squanto, and many Wampanoag did teach the Puritans how to farm corn, beans, and squash, rotate crops, maintain soil fertility, and survive in the harsh New England climate. So this first part of the Thanksgiving myth bears some truth.

However, there is no evidence of a tribal-white harvest celebration during the first Puritan winter in America in 1621. Although the Wampanoag, Pequot, and other Indians in the region routinely celebrated their fall harvest, the first evidence of a white-tribal harvest celebration appears in 1637. Also, it is an obvious romanticization to assume that the Indian-white relationship was all peace, hugs, and good eating. Metacom, also known as King Philip, was one of Massasoit's sons. In 1675, a chain of events led to a massive conflict sometimes called King Philip's War. Around 5 percent of the white population and 40 percent of the native population in the region was killed. Metacom's wife and children were sold as slaves in the West Indies, and the chief himself was killed by the Puritans. His head was placed on a pike and displayed in the village of Plymouth for more than twenty years.

The real Thanksgiving—it was complicated. Thanksgiving wasn't established as a holiday until the Civil War era and didn't become a formal federal holiday until 1941.

What is the real story of Pocahontas?

Soon after the establishment of Jamestown in 1607, Captain John Smith was captured by Opechancanough, the half brother of Wahunsenacawh (principal chief of the Powhatan Confederacy).[12] Wahunsenacawh's daughter, Pocahontas, helped Smith escape. Smith wrote about his captivity in 1608, 1612, and 1624, but only his last account mentioned that he was going to be executed before Pocahontas intervened, a clear embellishment.

In 1609, Captain John Ratcliffe demanded food tribute from the Powhatan, and when they resisted, he waged a sustained war against them from 1610 to 1614. Pocahontas was captured by the English in 1614 and ransomed to her father. The chief agreed to peace for her return, but the English continued to hold her and manipulate him. Pocahontas, still a teenager, was baptized and married to English planter John Rolfe (not John Smith), in spite of the fact that she was already married to a Powhatan man. Though she was never free to choose her relationship, she still wrestled with divided loyalties. She went to England with Rolfe, where her beauty brought her a great deal of attention, but she died, at age twenty-two, before she could return to America. Her son, Thomas Rolfe, survived and settled in Virginia, where some of his proven descendants still live today.

When did the U.S. government stop making treaties with Indians and why?

The United States established the right to make treaties in its earliest official configuration and codified that right in the U.S. constitution. The new country wanted to assert its sovereignty as it strove to become legitimate in the eyes of others. In both the constitution and early American history, treaties with Indians were the same as treaties with any other nation. But in 1871, a power struggle between the House and the Senate terminated the legislative power of the United States to treat with Indian nations.[13] Simply put, the House appropriated funds for Indian affairs but had no say in treaty making, while the Senate ratified treaties but did not hold the purse strings. When the Senate refused to engage both legislative houses in the treaty process, the House terminated the right to treat with tribes.

At this point, Indian treaties started to be handled differently from those made with other nations. New treaties to create incentives for removal could no longer be made. Congressional acts and executive orders—which were occasionally negotiated—sought to serve this function in the following decades. It seems counterintuitive that the United States would stop making treaties with Indians when there were still vast stretches of territory that had never been ceded, including more than three million acres around Upper and Lower Red Lakes in Minnesota alone. But there were many ways to get land from Indians, and the U.S. government made abundant use of these alternatives.

Why do some people use the word *genocide* in discussing the treatment of Indians?

The dictionary defines *genocide* as "the systematic killing of all the people from a national, ethnic, or religious group, or an attempt to do this."[14] The legal definition of genocide developed by the United Nations in 1948 is "any of the following acts committed with intent to destroy, in whole or in part, a national, ethnical, racial, or religious group, as such: killing members of the group; causing serious bodily or mental harm to members of the group; deliberately inflicting on the group conditions of life calculated to bring about its physical destruction in whole or in part; imposing measures intended to prevent births within the group; forcibly transferring children of the group to another group."[15] The reason that some people use the word *genocide* in discussing the treatment of Indians is that every single part of the dictionary and legal definitions of the word can be used to describe the historical treatment of Indians.

France attempted genocide on the Fox Indians in the 1730s, even refusing to allow women and children to surrender and issuing an official genocidal edict to back up their actions. During the French and Indian War, the British sent blankets infested with smallpox to tribes opposed to their colonization of the Great Lakes. Commander Lord Jeffrey Amherst instructed his subordinates to "inocculate the Indians by means of Blanketts, as well as to try Every other method that can serve to Extirpate this Execrable Race"; a recent outbreak had made blankets available, and by the next spring, tribes in the area were suffering from the disease.[16] The Russian, Spanish, and American colonial regimes all engaged in genocide toward the indigenous peoples of the Americas. In the United States, attempts to eradicate entire tribes had the greatest success in California, but other genocidal efforts were carried out across the country against the Apache, Lakota, and numerous other native nations. After the Dakota War of 1862, the tribal population in southern Minnesota was systematically hunted down, harried, relocated, and disrupted to the point where the state was almost completely depopulated of Dakota Indians. The present Dakota communities there have never fully recovered.

Even more recently, Indians have endured policies that fit the legal description of genocide, including the residential boarding school programs of the United States and Canada, the systematic removal of Indian children from their homes via social service practices, the ongoing wanton disregard for conditions of extreme poverty and homelessness in parts of Indian country, and the involuntary sterilization of Indian women by the U.S. Department of Health. (The U.S. government sterilized twenty-five thousand Indian women by tubal ligation without their consent in the 1960s and 1970s.[17]) *Genocide* might be the most honest word we have to describe these events.

Religion, Culture & Identity

"Indian time means that we will do your
ceremony until it's done. That's not an
excuse to be late or lazy."

THOMAS STILLDAY, Red Lake (Minnesota)

Why do Indians have long hair?

There are around five hundred distinct Indian tribes in North
America, and their cultural beliefs are diverse. For many Native
Americans, hair was viewed as a symbol of spiritual health and
strength. Leonard Moose, an Ojibwe elder from Mille Lacs, said
that hair was like medicine and if someone's hair was cut, his or
her medicine would leak out. Moose claimed that when he was a
child, if someone had a haircut, the parents would usually use a
hot rock to cauterize the wound on the child's hair and prevent
his or her medicine from draining away. Hair was a manifestation of spiritual strength or power but also a visible symbol of
that power, and thus a source of pride and even vanity. All of
these elements combine to provide a distinct cultural perspective about hair.

For most Indians, hair was only cut under certain circumstances. Meskwaki and Mohawk warriors plucked hair on the
sides of the head, a developing tradition in wars where scalping
was commonly practiced. Many Diné, or Navajo, cut children's
hair on their first birthday and then do not cut it again. They
believe that the purity of childhood preserves spiritual strength
and that the haircut will enable greater development of that
strength as the child grows. Among some tribes, hair was cut as

part of tribal mourning customs, but this practice was not universal. You can imagine how it must have felt for many native children to have their hair cut against their will upon entrance into U.S. government–run boarding schools (see page 138). Today, there are still many Native Americans who wear their hair long and carry the cultural belief that the hair is a symbol of spiritual strength.

Do Indians live in teepees?

Not usually. Europeans do not usually live in straw huts or ride horses as their primary means of transportation. And Indians do not usually live in historic dwellings or travel by foot, dogsled, or horse. Questions like these often speak to the mythologized fascination with Plains Indians, as seen in *Dances with Wolves* and other movies. We cannot hold onto a stereotype of how any people are and use that as the barometer for their authenticity.

Native Americans are diverse, and each group's practices have changed over time, but that does not diminish their authenticity. Today at sun dances, powwows, and other events, members of some Plains tribes set up tepees. The Iroquois use a longhouse for ceremonial functions. Many tribes in the Great Lakes use wigwams for ceremonies. In parts of the Southwest, hogans and pueblos are used for both ceremonial and everyday shelter.

What is fasting and why do Indians do it?

A *fast* is a search for a vision that will establish a relationship between the faster and the spiritual world. Many Indians believe the Great Spirit has a plan for everybody, and one never knows what it is, but fasting is a place where one can get a glimpse of it. By giving up food and water, the person who is fasting becomes disconnected from the physical world and more strongly connected to the spiritual world. This enhanced state enables a faster to be approached and "pitied" by spirits with the gift of a song, a medicine, the right to give Indian names, or the company of a guiding spirit.

For many tribes, a woman's power is her birthright, represented by her ability to bring life into the world through pregnancy and childbirth, and manifests when she comes of age. A man's spiritual power has to be earned through fasting. Males or females can fast any time of the year, but typically boys and young men are encouraged to fast, usually in the spring.

The process customarily begins by giving tobacco to someone who knows about fasting. That person will provide instructions on how to prepare and when to go. Young people are often given a choice about fasting. For some tribes, that choice might occur when a parent or namesake offers a child charcoal in one hand and breakfast or candy in the other. Children who choose the food are not ready. When they choose the charcoal, they are ready.

There are many differences in the methods of preparation and fasting. Some people might use a sweat lodge. Some fast on a platform, some on the ground, some in a lodge or in a tree. Occasionally people will fast with others, but usually it's a solitary activity.

It is possible to fast at any time of the year, but spring, a time of new life, is especially strong. Medicines are sprouting, birds and animals are coming back from migration or out of hibernation. Physically and spiritually, the world is coming alive. It's possible to fast at any age, but fasts are most common in the spring of one's life, when it is easier to earn pity from the spirits. Adults have to sit out longer to make the same connections.

What are clans and do all Indians have them?

Clans, or totems, are birds, animals, fish, or spiritual beings or places that represent different families in many native communities. Most tribes have clan systems. At Cochiti Pueblo there are two essential groupings—Turquoise and Pumpkin. Those groupings matter a great deal for the organization of some dances but do not function like the clan systems of other tribes. Many, including the Plains tribes, have maintained sophisticated kin networks without clan systems. Others, like the Dakota, used to maintain clan systems and kinship networks but have since lost and discontinued this practice. For most of the tribes in the Algonquian and Iroquoian language families, clans remain a critical part of tribal life. In Iroquoian tribes, tribal members follow their mother's clan. The clan system is even incorporated into the rights of tribal members to participate in ceremonial longhouse doings. Ojibwe people follow the clan of their fathers. Forest County Potawatomi boys follow the clan of the father and girls follow the clan of the mother.[1]

For tribes that maintain beliefs in clan, it is customarily taboo to marry someone of the same clan. There are ingrained cultural concepts that vary from tribe to tribe for handling situations where one has a nonnative parent from whom they would normally receive their clan. Some believe there is an automatic adoption into a certain clan or a necessary ceremony or ritual to obtain a clan for the person who needs one.

Where are the real Indians?

Once, when I was lecturing in France, a man in the back of the room raised his hand with great excitement. French guys never get excited at academic talks, so I took his question. And his question was, "Where are the real Indians?" I suppose he was looking for someone who just stepped off the set for *Dances with Wolves*. I replied, "Where are the real Indians? Where are the real Frenchmen? There is a castle across the street, and there is nobody living in it. In fact, I don't see anybody riding up and down the street on horses with shining armor. I don't even see guys with berets and little pipes. Where are the real Frenchmen?"

All cultures change over time. What it meant to be French a thousand years ago, a hundred years ago, and today are all different. But a Frenchman can still be French even if he's traveling in China because he carries that identity inside of him. It's the same for Indians, who carry their identity with them. Many different things inform identity, including heredity, connection to tribal communities, traditional lifeways, and tribal languages. Each of those dimensions of identity might be threatened for many Indian people, but what it means to be Indian is both complicated and very real, in spite of the presuppositions engendered by movies and stereotypes.

What does *traditional* mean?

That's a loaded question. Defining tradition is a very subjective process. People from Pittsburgh who happen to be of German heritage might have a very different idea of what is traditional compared to the Pennsylvania Amish. Tradition is about much more than biology. Because cultures, languages, technologies, and values shift far faster than most people realize, it is hard to define what is truly traditional.

For Indians, defining what is traditional gets further tied up in a sometimes-contested discussion of identity. For example, the community of Ponemah on the Red Lake Reservation in Minnesota has 100 percent traditional Ojibwe religious belief and funerary practice. No one has ever been baptized in that community. And the fluency rate in the tribal language there is the highest of all Ojibwe communities in the United States. Across the lake, in the community of Red Lake, on the same reservation, the tribal population is predominantly Catholic. People in Ponemah define tradition by religion, traditional lifeways, and language. But people from Red Lake tend to emphasize heredity (blood), hunting and fishing, and reservation affiliation as more central dimensions of identity, Indianness, and tradition.

This example demonstrates how contested political discussions of tradition can be. Personally, I find the customs, practices, language, and beliefs of my ancestors to be defining features of tradition and central to my identity. But I also live in a modern world. I drive a car and wear manufactured clothing.

Although my life differs from those of my ancestors of a few hundred years ago, I find much more in common with them in my own religious choices, cultural beliefs and practices, and language. I tried to make that distinction to the Frenchman who asked about where the real Indians were (page 42), but it is important to recognize that the tension between old and new, modern and traditional, is ongoing and intense in Indian country.

Aren't all Indians traditional?

There is incredible diversity in Indian country. There are communities in Canada and remote parts of the Navajo reservation where fluency rates in native languages approach 100 percent. In many other communities, there are no speakers left. Some communities have 100 percent traditional religious and funerary belief. There are also some communities in which all members have converted to Christianity. Each place has its own his-

Billboard on the road to Ponemah (Red Lake Nation)

tory. And it is usually through no fault of their own that many Indians do not speak their tribal languages. At the same time, while many forces and realities are beyond the control of any individual human being or community, there are some things Indians can exercise more control over. And, fair or not, it is necessarily up to native people to take steps to stabilize traditional custom, practice, and language.

In the Upper Midwest, almost 30 percent of the nonnative population is of German heritage. But their families have lived in the United States for as long as five generations. They don't speak the German language and have never lived in Germany. In fact, if you sent them to Germany, they might have a nice vacation, but they would be most comfortable when they came home to the United States. There is a difference between having German heritage and being a Deutschlander. And so too is there a big difference between having native heritage and being Apsáalooke, or Crow. I believe strongly in the importance of tribal language, although I'm not so much of a fundamentalist as to say that non-speakers are not Indian. But the more divorced Indians become from tribal language, culture, religion, and custom, the more unrecognizable we become to our ancestors. How much can a people change before they are no longer the same people?

Why is it called a "traditional Indian fry bread taco"?

That question is as befuddling to me as "Where do the wood ticks go during the wintertime?" There is a traditional fry bread taco stand at every single powwow and many other secular and social events. Frankly, the words *traditional, Indian, fry bread,* and *taco* do not have any business even being in the same sentence. Taco? Really? Fry bread was created by resourceful Indians who were trying to subsist upon U.S. government rations of lard and flour. It is certainly not traditional. Indians laugh at the irony, and I know I'm a sucker for one of those once in a while myself. But Indians need to wake up to the harsh realities of the world.

Ironic and humorous though it might seem, given that we have the highest rate of diabetes for any racial group in the world, mislabeling this concoction as "traditional" is killing us.

What is Indian time?

"Indian time" is another terrible misconception widely held in Indian country. Today the concept is used as an excuse to be late or lazy. But Native Americans in former times were neither. If you woke up late or took a lazy day, your children often went hungry. People worked hard and were physically fit in order to survive. In former times, Indians also worried a great deal about "bad medicine" and had a level of fear and respect that modified behavior. People did not show up late for social or ceremonial events out of fear that doing so might offend someone who had the power to do spiritual harm to others.

Mille Lacs Ojibwe elder Melvin Eagle once told me that when he was a child, he and a friend were playing and laughing in a road and an old man walking by thought they were laughing at him. He told his mother, who immediately made him take tobacco and gifts to the old man's residence to apologize and explain that he was not laughing at the old man. This care of relationships, like being on time, is a mark of respect. Today, among some people I see a lack of work ethic and respect that would have horrified any Indian from a couple hundred years ago. According to Red Lake Ojibwe elder Thomas Stillday, *Indian time* simply means that we will do your ceremony until your ceremony is done, no matter how long it takes, with no shortcuts.[2] It is not an excuse to be late or lazy.

What are Indian cars?

Regardless of what may have happened in recent years, when we look back to BC (Before Casinos), most Native Americans shared the experience of impoverishment. The good and bad vestiges of that suffering permeate Indian communities today, even in places where poverty is less of a concern. The Indian car has been viewed by many as a symbolic manifestation of the shared experience of poverty. The Indian car is the one that is falling apart—its bumper is held on with duct tape and bailing wire, and the tires are all brothers from different marriages. I have a couple of cars in my yard that meet this description, but those vehicles are not defining features of who I am. And I make that distinction with purpose.

Today in Indian country, there is an incorrectly but widely held view that to suffer in poverty is to be authentically Indian. While poverty was a common experience, the negative dimensions of the culture of poverty are at odds with older, traditional indigenous views of self. Pictures taken in the nineteenth century show people wearing decent pants and beautiful beadwork. They took pride in their personal appearance. They dressed up, especially for ceremony. Now, many Indians dress down, wearing jeans and t-shirts and leaving their beadwork in the closet when it's ceremony time, for fear they will be labeled as stuck-up or seen as showing off. While the native talent in artistry

Ojibwe Indians at White Earth, 1886

and beadwork is proudly on display at the modern powwow, it is absent from almost every other dimension of tribal life.

People dress down and celebrate their poverty because they mistakenly view an expression of poverty as an expression of Indianness. Our ancestors traditionally sought to improve their standard of living through hard work and personal pride in trade, diplomacy, and trapping. Today's embrace of the culture of poverty is at odds with the world view of our ancestors.

I thought that Indians have a strong sense of ecological stewardship, so why do I also see a lot of trash in some yards?

If we were all true to the religious and cultural principles of our forebears, there would be many fewer problems in the world. The Bible has a lot of teachings about peace, but many Christians actively participate in war and have done so consistently for two thousand years. It is true that many native value systems and religious beliefs espouse a deep respect for all animate and inanimate things. No matter how modest one's dwelling might be, traditional belief systems emphasize keeping it clean and treating it with respect. Although the sense of environmental stewardship attributed to Indians is sometimes romanticized, there is an authentic value of respect and reciprocity in native interactions with the natural world.

At the same time, Indians, like all human beings, have sought to advance their position and make life easier for themselves, occasionally resulting in divergence between belief and practice. Pressures on Indian land and livelihoods and European demands for furs all contributed to an indigenous practice of harvesting beaver to extinction in some areas. Native Americans in the southern Great Lakes intentionally set forest fires to extend the range of the woodland buffalo eastward all the way to New Jersey. These actions created easier access to critical food supplies, and while they had a positive impact on the population of buffalo, they worked to the detriment of certain other flora and fauna. Controlled fires also created fire breaks to protect villages from wildfires (and forests from village cooking fires) and to enhance the productivity of certain crops such as blueberries. *Changes in the Land* by William Cronon and *1491* by Charles Mann do a great job of describing the ways that American Indians made their environments.

Trash bothers me, too, but the issue of trash in people's yards speaks to a larger concern. There has been a systematic attempt to assimilate Native Americans, and the effects of assimilation, historical trauma, and poverty have served to erode traditional values of respect and pride in personal appearance and residence. Possessing fancy clothes, cars, houses, and other displays of wealth does not mean that one is more respected in Indian country. But in many native communities the traditional value and belief is that, no matter how humble or extravagant the dwelling, good spirits are attracted to clean places and bad spirits hide under clutter and garbage. When I see garbage in someone's yard, I am more likely to view it as an indication of acculturation than the degree to which traditional Indian values are environmentally sensitive. For me, Indians who do not keep their homes or yards clean are out of touch with these ancient yet important traditional values.

I see this issue as a reflection of the deeper one of poverty in Indian country. All disproportionately poor subsections of the population have a similar issue. Those who do not own their homes take less pride in their residences. Many tribes manage their own garbage and recycling programs and coordinate youth activities to clean up their communities. Tribes are doing their best to address this issue. Cultural values lend great support to that effort. But there's still plenty of work to do.

Do Indians have a stronger sense of community than non-Indians?

Definitely. For most Americans, living in this country has meant dislocating from motherland and mother tongue. An American

can move from the East Coast to the West and shift from being a New Yorker to being a Californian. Identity has become malleable. Native Americans have a stronger tether and bond to community. Even most Native Americans who leave their home reservations to work in cities will frequently travel home for family and community functions. And regardless of personal religious choice, it is exceptionally rare for Indians to have a funeral outside of their home community, even if they've spent most of their life living off-reservation.

Some places have an especially strong sense of community. In Ponemah, on the Red Lake Reservation, no individuals own land. All land is held in federal trust for the benefit of all tribal members. Homesteads are established for families that live on the reservation, but those families cannot own the land on which they live. This situation makes it hard to get a loan for a house, but it has maintained a strong sense of community. The rights to homestead in a particular place are passed down through families. Almost all of the families on that reservation are living on plots of land that their parents and grandparents and great-grandparents, going back through generations, have lived on. Further, in Ponemah, the custom is to bury one's dead relatives in the front yard. There are often many generations buried in every front yard—which makes it a lot harder to sell the family farm and move to California. And although not every single member of every single family attends every funeral, at least *someone* from every family attends local funerals and brings food. They do this not just because they knew the person, which, given a community numbering one thousand, they usually do. They do it simply because they are members of the same community. The Pueblos also have a remarkably strong sense of community. When there is a dance or feast day, every family participates without question or resistance.

What is Indian religion?

Because there is so much diversity in Indian country, there is no such thing as "Indian religion." Customs and traditions vary significantly from tribe to tribe. In the Great Lakes and other regions, some tribes have societies that require a religious initiation. Such initiations are conducted entirely according to ancient tribal customs but function much like baptism and confirmation do for Christians. Those ceremonies serve to place the initiates on a particular religious path and are often accompanied by instructions and expectations for a certain code of conduct. Other tribes have societies that are spiritual in nature but do not serve to induct someone into a particular religious belief system. For most tribes, though, religious belief is less focused upon specific ceremonies or induction into specific groups than on a set of values, beliefs, and rituals that are infused into everyday life. As such, Indian religion, spiritual perspective, and custom tend to be organic, somewhat fluid, and integrated rather than exclusive.

Indian religious practices were forbidden by the federal government in 1883, and parts of those regulations were not formally repealed until 1978. Many Indians became Christians of various denominations, and others have adopted aspects of Christianity. An organization called the Native American Church incorporates traditional pre-Columbian use of peyote with Christianity. Other Indian religious rituals have infused ideas, values, or even customs of Christianity with tribal practice.

Why do Indians use tobacco for ceremonies?

Most tribal communities in North America use tobacco. Although customs vary from tribe to tribe, most Indians believe that any spiritual request made of the Creator or one's fellow human beings must be "paid" for. Tobacco is viewed as an item of not just economic but primarily spiritual value. It is a reciprocal offering. Some tribes, including all of the Pueblos, also use cornmeal with this same view in mind.

Isaac Treuer offering tobacco

Some tribes, such as the Potawatomi and Ho-Chunk (Winnebago), cultivate their own tobacco. Other tribes make "tobacco" from other plants and medicines, especially the inner bark of red willow or dogwood. Often red willow tobacco is mixed with other medicines or cultivated tobacco to form kinnickinnick. Indian people who practice traditional religious beliefs and customs differentiate between the use of spiritual tobacco and the abuse of chemical-laden pleasure tobacco. When tobacco is used in ceremony, generally it is the least carcinogenic form and the smoking does not involve inhalation, somewhat mitigating potential health risks.

It seems like Indians have a deeper spiritual connection than in many religious traditions. Is that true?

Most Indian religious traditions are far less hierarchical, structured, or driven by rigid organization than Judeo-Christian religious forms, making association and practice more fluid, natural, and easily obtained for practitioners. For example, Christians rely upon the Bible to acquire moral teachings and religious belief. Someone who is not baptized is often denied or at least discouraged from participating in communion.

For many participants in Indian spirituality, there is no dogmatic set of principles to govern their knowledge of the Creator. It is far more likely that someone would go fasting to obtain a vision and rely upon that vision for their deeper understanding of the Creator and their relationship with the Almighty. There is much less power placed in the hands of a native spiritual leader than in a pope, bishop, priest, or other religious official. Indian religious leaders do have status and often receive a high degree of respect from people in their community. But if somebody does not like what they hear or the substance of any particular religious form in Indian country, they are free to disassociate without significantly diminishing their access to their religion or their status as a religious person among their peers. The same freedom does not exist for Catholics, for example, who would have a hard time practicing their faith without attending mass.

Access to genuine spiritual connection can be a frustrating part of the human experience for all people, including Indians, especially those living in urban communities or places where traditional religious practice has become severely depleted or assimilated. Those frustrations are somewhat mitigated by the fact that for most Indians, prayer is not a weekly event arranged by others but a daily event that is self-orchestrated. Further, access to more complicated ceremonies and free expression at those ceremonies is less regimented for many native people.

What are some of the customs around pregnancy and childbirth?

Customs vary so much from tribe to tribe that it is difficult to give an answer that represents the breadth and depth of belief and practice. It is the prevailing belief of many Indian people that we do not have souls. Rather, we are souls. We have bodies. In fact, our bodies are but temporary houses for our souls. The terms *soul* and *spirit* are used interchangeably. The Ojibwe word for *body, niiyaw,* literally means "my vessel." The body is a container.

Many tribes believe that when a woman is pregnant, the spirit of her unborn child is hovering around her body. The fetus inside of her does not yet house the baby's soul; the spirit of the child has not yet fully arrived. For this reason, there are many taboos when a woman is pregnant.

Another commonly held belief in the Great Lakes region is that the spirit of the child actually chooses his or her parents. That spirit then comes to earth to hover around his or her mother while she's carrying the fetus, the body that he or she will inhabit upon birth. This belief is often strongly impressed upon young people as they themselves become parents, showing them the Indian way of thinking about their spiritual responsibility.

Many Native Americans believe the Great Spirit has a plan for everyone. The Great Spirit's plan has a profound impact and influence on everyone's life. We never know what the Great Spirit's plan is, but we can get glimpses of it through dreams and visions while sleeping or fasting. At the same time, there are also forces of random luck both good and bad. Sometimes people die before their time. Sometimes people live beyond their time. The world is not fair. But it is our belief that when we follow the teachings of our ancestors and tread upon the earth with respect, we have a greater chance of seeing the Great Spirit's plan realized. Traditional elders often admonish their relatives not to interfere with the Great Spirit's plan. This is one of the reasons why something like murder is not accepted in many tribal cultures. We do not know better than the Great Spirit when someone's time should end. Many Indians choose not to have abortions because of this common belief.

In former times, there was a much higher rate of infant mortality. Because a small baby's hold on life is tenuous, many customs seek to show the spirits that the family is grateful for the arrival of their new child but does not assume that a gift is given before it comes. For example, people in Indian country usually do not have a baby shower before the child is born; doing so would show the spirits that the family assumes the child will arrive and live. Such assumptions are not only out of keeping with traditional teachings; they can also lead to incredible grief should there be misfortune with the pregnancy or childbirth. In keeping with this view, Earl Otchingwanigan (Michigan) and other elders have often said that the cradleboard for a family's firstborn should not be made until the child is four weeks

Luella Treuer in a cradleboard, January 2012. The cradleboard entertains an infant while keeping the child safe.

old. Once the cradleboard has been made, it becomes a family heirloom, and it can be passed from the first to the second to the third child without any fear of negative consequences or assumptions.

It is widely believed that when a woman is pregnant, the hovering spirit of the baby is very vulnerable. Expectant mothers are told to be careful of what they say, as it can invite good or bad luck. In some tribes, mothers are told not to look at salamanders, snakes, or even cats. Many families instruct expectant mothers not to eat burnt food. Everything an expectant mother consumes affects her baby, including well-known things, such as drugs or alcohol, but also traditional foods. Too many strawberries or blueberries might give the child blue or red marks on his or her body.

Expectant mothers in many tribes are also urged not to attend funerals. The spiritual process for the arrival of her child is the exact opposite of that for the departure of someone who passed away. The two don't mix. Everybody loves a brand-new baby—even departing souls love brand-new babies. Out of fear that the departing soul at a funeral might want to take a sweet baby with him or her, expectant mothers simply stay away. Even young children are usually kept away from funerals. If a child's presence at a funeral cannot be avoided, the custom for many tribes is to rub charcoal on his or her forehead. This is a "passover," so the departing soul will not see or disturb the child. It is believed that failing to mark a passover could cause bad dreams for the child or possibly invite the child's own departure from the earth.

There is a great deal of variation in regional customs around childbirth. According to Ojibwe spiritual leader Archie Mosay (Wisconsin), the parents made a tea out of catnip, called *namewashk* in Ojibwe, in order to give the new baby his or her first bath. This plant grows abundantly throughout the region, is picked in the summer, and can be dried. Once the tea is made, the liquid is strained. Some families also lay the baby on a bed of moss. It is believed that in so doing the child will be bonded with Mother Earth.

Many native families save the placenta and bring it home. There are a few different customs around proper treatment of the placenta. According to Ojibwe elder Leonard Moose, the placenta should be put up in the east side of a white pine tree. The white pine is a symbol of wisdom and longevity, and east is the direction from which the sun, the source of all life, rises. According to Ojibwe elder Earl Otchingwanigan, the placenta should be buried on the north side of a maple tree. The maple tree is the tree of life, and north is the direction at the end of the cycle. With all of these customs, tobacco is put out with the placenta.

A week or two after the umbilical cord has been cut, the dried end of the cord falls off of the baby, and it is often placed in a small pouch. If the child is being kept in a cradleboard much of the time, the pouch is hung on the crash bar for the cradleboard. If the child spends more time in an Indian swing, the pouch is tied onto the swing. If the child uses neither a cradleboard nor a swing, the pouch can be hung on the wall near where he or she sleeps. After one year, the spiritual connection between the baby and his or her umbilical cord fades. It can be kept as a memento, but the cord serves no physical or spiritual function. It is said that babies who did not have their cord and belly button saved for a year will spend the rest of their lives "looking for it." They might want to open cupboards in strangers' houses or look through other people's medicine cabinets. It is believed that this habit is derived from the denial of connection to one's belly button. We become emotionally attached to anything that we see or touch extensively, as in the umbilical cord in the womb. The attachment a child has to his or her cord simply fades over time.

What are naming ceremonies?

Obtaining an Indian name is one of the most basic yet treasured customs in Indian country. Traditions vary from tribe to
tribe, but there are some commonalities as well. Indian names
are given in tribal languages, with very few exceptions. Many
tribal members believe these are the languages of the spirits,
who give the names through people. For many tribes, including
the Ho-Chunk, Meskwaki, Dakota, Lakota, and others, there is
an ancestral connection in the giving of a name. Parents do not
usually pick the name for their child; rather, the parents pick a
spiritual leader to bestow a name upon their child. For tribes
where the ancestral connection is critical, the giving of a name
creates a strong and lifelong relationship between the person
receiving it and an ancestor who has gone on to the spirit world.

Other tribes, such as the Ojibwe, do not usually have an ancestor connection in the giving of a name. For them, names
come from spirits, not from people. Those who officiate at naming ceremonies are more like translators. Name givers speak to
the spirits and the people. They translate. The names are usually obtained from fasting or dreams, and each name has a story
behind it. Someone might see a vision or have a dream about a
giant bear descending through the clouds and give the name
"Bear." Some Ojibwe chiefs have used public names, in addition
to their spirit names, that suited their purposes. Bagone-giizhig
(Hole in the Day) and some other Minnesota Ojibwe chiefs even
used their fathers' names to capitalize on their recognition and
prestige.

Many Ojibwe tribal elders instruct people to have a feast four
days after the birth of a child. The purpose of this first feast
is to welcome the arrival of a new spirit in the world. In some
places, the naming ceremony is performed at this feast. For others, it happens later. Both parents have equal say about choos-
ing a name giver. The only requirement for name givers in most
tribal traditions is that they have an Indian name themselves.

However, no matter who is running a naming ceremony,

some ideas about traditional Indian names are universal. Indian names are spiritual identification—how spirits know people. The Ojibwe word for body, *niiyaw*, literally means "my vessel." The body is a container. This word is reflected in other Ojibwe words, like *niiyawe'enh*, meaning "my namesake," a term used interchangeably for both the name giver and the name receiver because the meaning describes the way a name giver puts part of himself into his young namesake and the namesake's body becomes a housing for part of the name giver's spirit. The namesake relationship is for life. But a namesake is more than just the person who gives a name. A namesake acts as an adviser, guide, and role model, much like a godparent in other traditions. Namesakes are important in other ceremonies throughout life.

Usually, if someone wants to ask for spiritual help, he or she must personally approach a wise person and give tobacco. But when namesakes take tobacco, they are making a lifetime commitment. Later in life, someone can call his or her namesake and ask for spiritual help, even if the namesake has moved far away. Because namesakes accept tobacco on the day of the naming, they can smoke their pipes and pray for their namesakes.

Can a nonnative person get an Indian name?

In many tribal customs, Indian names can be bestowed upon anyone, regardless of race. The custom is open and widely shared. However, this practice is not universal among all tribal communities. For some, names come from specific ancestors and cannot be given to someone who is not a lineal descendant. For others, names come from ancestors and can go to anyone, but family members are reluctant to give such a special personal honor to an outsider. Some tribes, like the Hopi and Pueblo, used to be more open to outsiders but got overrun by curiosity seekers; they have made many of their cultural displays and practices more exclusive to protect their sanctity and to ease access for their own people.

If a non-Indian person wishes to obtain an Indian name, he or she should simply offer tobacco to a knowledgeable spiritual leader and ask what the custom is in that area. And should the answer be that Indian names are only given to Indian people in that community, he or she should respect the existing traditions.

What are coming-of-age ceremonies?

As in many cultures, adolescence is a special and empowering time in a person's life. Customs vary from one tribe to another and are also usually very different for boys and girls.

In Indian country, menstruation is universally seen as a representation of the spiritual power of women and their ability to bring life into the world. This view is quite different from common cultural beliefs in mainstream society that often leave adolescent girls feeling dirty or embarrassed when their change of life occurs. For many tribes, a woman's spiritual power in relation to other spiritual powers is similar to the repelling effect of trying to push together two magnets: it's not bad, but it needs to be given its own space.

When a girl gets her first "moon," she is infused with this positive spiritual power. It is a common belief that the power is so great that it could interfere with other beings, other processes that are in the world. In former times throughout the Great Lakes area, when a girl got her first moon, she was sequestered in her own wigwam. It's difficult to do that today, so tribal members who follow traditional customs make accommodations. A girl might spend more time in her bedroom or another safe, private place. In times past, this separation was enforced in a very strict way—young women were secluded from men, from sacred items, and from many kinds of ceremonies. During this time, grandmothers and female namesakes gave her instructions on how to conduct herself as a woman.

Most Great Lakes tribes instruct girls to use their own dish and spoon every time they get their period for the year after first menses. Some use this dish and spoon throughout the first year. This practice teaches about how powerful they are and how to use restraint, how to be aware of their actions. Most girls store their special dishes in a bundle separate from other household items. Other commonly followed rules for the entire first year as a woman include: don't go swimming, don't go in the water, don't step over anything, don't handle men's belongings, don't touch anything growing—new life, brand-new babies, or puppies.

This is the start of the time when a girl can have a baby. She is instructed about the physical changes to her body and her rights and responsibilities as a woman. During her first year, an Ojibwe girl can't eat traditional foods until a feast is held where someone feeds her that season's food as it is harvested. The feast offers protection to the harvests: the woman's power is so great that if she eats the fresh wild rice, or blueberries, or fish without a feast she could affect the crop in that area.

Once the final food is fed to an Ojibwe girl at the end of her first year as a woman, there is a more elaborate ceremony during which all the women, including her extended family and her female namesakes, come to give teachings. These lessons might include

* * * * *

You are a woman now. So, if you see a bunch of us sitting around, you come sit with us. You are one of us.

You are a woman now, so you have a right and a responsibility to be respected by men. What that means is

No one can hit you;

No one can call you names;

No one can make you do something sexually that you don't want to do.

Look around at your ceremonies. You'll see that there are jobs for women and for men. There is a place for women at ceremonies. Those places at those ceremonies show that balance of men and women.

If something cannot avoid being touched, you can use gloves to alleviate the possibility of your power interfering with the spirit power of anything else.

Cedar is a powerful medicine. It can be used as a smudge, as a tea, to sit on, in your shoes, even in your underwear. It acts as a barrier.

Refrain from most ceremonies. Stay back as far as possible. Exceptions are sometimes made for the most important and longest ceremonies, with added cautions.

Use your skirt. It is your spiritual identification as a woman. You should be proud of your womanhood. Just as cedar provides a barrier, if something is going to drop, your skirt provides that barrier and channels it down to the ground.

You will be cautioned to watch your skirt to make sure it doesn't go over people or food.

After the first year is up, you don't have to eat on separate dishes anymore, but your spiritual power remains tremendous every time you have your moon.

* * * * *

Sometimes this training is misunderstood by those outside the cultural practice as an assertion of uncleanliness for menstruating women. But the indoctrination of girls into the ranks of womanhood is accompanied by such strong and consistent reinforcements of positive power, right, and responsibility that the perception and practice in Indian country is one of empowerment.

Boys often receive instructions on their transition to manhood as part of a private experience while fasting soon after their voice begins to change. However, the transition to manhood in many tribal customs can also be associated with the assumption of responsibilities as a provider for the people by hunting, fishing, trapping, and snaring.

In most tribes, both boys and girls can harvest wild game. A person's first successful hunt is usually a time of ceremony marking the transition to adulthood. The Ojibwe call the ceremony *oshki-nitaagewin*. Boys may be groomed a little more for it, but girls do *oshki-nitaagewin* too. The word means "to make a kill for the first time," and the ceremony may be repeated for the first rabbit, fish, partridge, and deer.

When one first kills an animal, there is almost always an offering of tobacco. The hunter will actually speak to the animal killed. An effort is made to show the animal that he wasn't simply killed for sport. The animal has given up his life so that the people can eat, a self-sacrifice. It is usually taboo to waste one's kill. There are regional variations, but many animals have a part that is considered special, that houses the animal's spirit. This part will be put out with tobacco. Some families cook the whole deer and invite the entire village when someone makes a first kill. It is now more common for a family to make accommodations for modern life by cooking some of the deer and then packaging up the rest to give away.

At most first-kill feasts, tobacco is shared. The people smoke. Someone approaches the hunter and takes a spoon of meat and offers the first bite to him, saying his Indian name. But the hunter has to refuse the first bite. Some people will offer it four times, and on the fourth time he can eat.

Ojibwe elder Mary Roberts (Manitoba) instructed young people to say something on the first refusal of the offered food: "No, I'm thinking of the children who have no one to provide for them." The food is returned to the pot, a new piece of meat is taken and offered, and the hunter refuses again, saying, "No, I'm thinking of elders who can't get out into the woods to hunt for themselves." The food is put back and a third spoonful is offered, and again he refuses: "No, I'm thinking of the people who came here today to support me." When offered a fourth bite of the food, he can eat it. Then the hunter is told, "You just changed your life. You are now a provider for the people. And every time you kill an animal, these are the things you think about: children who have no one providing for them, elders who can't feed themselves, your family, community, and supporters. And to reinforce this, you now have to give away your entire remaining kill. You are not hunting for glory. You are hunting for food and to provide for your family and community. It's important that you have respect for your family and the animals." The young hunter is then thanked with hugs and handshakes and formally acknowledged as having transitioned from dependent to provider.

How come everyone's laughing at a traditional Indian funeral?

Not everyone is laughing. Grief is real and difficult for people of all cultures. But for many tribes, belief in the afterlife is deeply held. Unlike funerary customs for many Judeo-Christian traditions, a death does not provide an opportunity for a priest to preach at the bereaved so much as it provides the family an opportunity to share with the dead. Food, songs, prayers, and instructions on how to reach the spirit world are given to the deceased. The process is often long and complicated, but it heightens the sense of a departing soul's arrival in the spirit world, respect for tradition, and celebration of a life lived and an even better destination for the departing soul. People grieve at traditional funerals, too, but the grief is mitigated by the spiritual process and ritual. Community and family support is usually very pronounced. In many native communities, all families, even those not of immediate relation, cook and bring food to wakes and funerals.

The Ojibwe bury their dead in shallow graves, put holes in the rough box and casket, and even add holes to the spirit house which is placed over the burial site, all to enable the soul to visit its body. But after four years all of this fades and the spirit house is allowed to disintegrate and return to earth. Since the spirit of the departed is believed to be emotionally attached to its vessel, this gives time for the attachment to dissipate.

Do they charge for participation in native ceremonies?

For the most part, only charlatans do that. Mille Lacs elder James Clark once told me, "If you give someone a dollar for a ceremony, the spirits will look at it and think that it's a pretty small blanket." Most ceremonies involve a ritual gift of tobacco. For more important ceremonies, there is usually a food offering and a cloth item such as a blanket. More elaborate ceremonies may involve other types of gifts, clothing, and sacred items.

Customs vary a lot from ceremony to ceremony and tribe to tribe, but money is a new physical item and cultural concept, so its use in ceremony is usually uncommon. There are some occasions, such as ceremonial drums, where members may give money in lieu of a homemade or store-purchased gift, but that is different from charging others for helping them. Sometimes spiritual leaders travel great distances at personal expense to assist others, and those seeking their help may give them gas money, but that is also different from charging a fee. Most tribal members view charging for ceremony as "bad form," and some even consider it taboo.

What is a sweat lodge?

A sweat lodge is a small, dome-shaped frame made out of tree saplings that is covered with bark, mats, blankets, or canvas. Rocks are heated in a fire outside of the lodge and brought inside. Water is poured on the rocks similar to the function of a sauna. Many Indians use sweat lodges to pray and sometimes incorporate medicines for healing or use it as a purification ritual in preparation for fasting, Sun Dance, or other ceremonies. The sweat lodge ceremony is one of the most well-known and widely practiced Indian ceremonies today. As a result, there is a great deal of variation in practice.

Sometimes the ceremony has been copied or even abused by outsiders. In October 2009, a white man named James Arthur Ray charged money to nonnative people to participate in an "authentic Indian sweat lodge ceremony" in Sedona, Arizona. He had dozens of people packed into a small lodge and kept it too hot for too long. Three people died: Kirby Brown, James Shore, and Liz Neuman. Ray was convicted on three counts of negligent homicide.[3] In this case it seems quite clear that the person running the ceremony was an irresponsible charlatan who preyed on the emotional and spiritual vulnerabilities of nonnative people fascinated with Indian spirituality. I see his actions as criminal and spiritually reprehensible. Sweat lodges are commonly used by true native spiritual leaders from many communities, but the physical experience never endangers human life when done responsibly and when the event is carried out with a true desire to help others rather than profit from their needs.

Do Indians still get persecuted for their religious beliefs?

Yes. In 1883, the U.S. commissioner of Indian Affairs created a "Code of Indian Offenses" that was used to persecute tribal religious practice.[4] Until 1933, Circular 1665 instructed Indian agents to ban and break up tribal dances, religious ceremonies, and giveaways, even after Indians became U.S. citizens in 1924. The first amendment to the U.S. constitution was insufficient to provide for the religious freedom of Indians the way it did for Americans of other races. In 1978, the American Indian Religious Freedom Act sought to remedy that.

However, even today, free practice of religious custom is sometimes elusive. In 2008, Damien Bad Boy, an enrolled member and resident of the White Earth Reservation (Minnesota), was continually harassed by the city of Mahnomen, which claimed that his sweat lodge (located on his private property) violated city building codes, fire codes, and noise ordinances. Bad Boy pursued legal action and eventually settled a civil suit out of court. The city has never changed its laws or sought to negotiate with the tribe to allow for traditional sweat lodge use.

His case was not unique. An Indian in Tennessee had his sweat lodge destroyed by the local fire department several times in the 1980s. And many tribes and tribal members cannot access their own sacred sites or sacred items. Peyote use for tribes that incorporate it in ceremonies and for the more modern Native American Church remains a contentious and sometimes restricted practice. Native Americans in federal or state prisons are often only allowed access to Judeo-Christian religious leaders. Tobacco and traditional medicines are not allowed in prisons or most schools. Although conditions have certainly improved over the past century, there are many ways in which free practice of ancient custom remains difficult for Indians.

Powwow

"So you want me to choose between
going to powwows and being with you.
Well, I made up my mind. Come here
pretty darling, give me a kiss goodbye."

OJIBWE SONG BY PIPESTONE SINGERS

What is a powwow?

The word *powwow* is actually derived from a term for spiritual leader in the Narragansett and Massachusett languages but was later misapplied to many types of ceremonial and secular events. Although Ojibwe drum ceremonies and traditional Dakota wacipi dances sometimes are referred to as *powwows*, today's events are commonly secular, not ceremonial, and are widely practiced all over North America. They usually last anywhere from one to three days, and they are open to people of all tribes, genders, ages, and races. Powwows are primarily dance events, where people wear sometimes elaborate beadwork, feathers, and other regalia and dance to a wide array of songs performed by numerous drum groups, each comprised of anywhere from five to twenty singers. The powwow is a relatively new cultural form, although one of the most vibrant in all of Indian country.[1]

Many tribes from the Northern Plains and Great Lakes had different types of drum ceremonies and war dances at the time of first contact with Europeans. From these ceremonies evolved a more secular dance that often involved people from many different tribes. It used to be that each eagle feather worn by an Indian represented a deed done in battle—a kill, wound, or scalp—so wearing a feather bonnet, bustle, or dog soldier hat marked one as a fearsome warrior. Often, warriors and chiefs proudly displayed their feathers at treaty signings and diplomatic events, showing their military might, parading into the compounds of U.S. Army forts, for example. This custom evolved into the current *grand entry*, where Indians of all ages and genders parade into the dance arbor, although it is still veterans who lead. Styles of dance from the Omaha (grass dance), Dakota (war dance), Ojibwe (jingle dress), and other tribes were freely shared across tribal lines.

In the 1960s and 1970s, tribal governments in many places began to devote financial resources to support powwows, encouraging participation by providing meals and even money to dancers and singers. The custom grew into sometimes extravagant displays and even competitions with prize purses for best singing and dancing in multiple categories. Some of the wealthiest tribes, such as the Mashantucket Pequot, sponsored powwows with a total prize purse of more than $1 million. Even less well-off tribes like Leech Lake (Minnesota) have devoted hundreds of thousands of dollars to support powwow customs. The practice is vibrant because an overwhelming majority of the tribal population participates in powwows, and the custom transcends lines of religious choice, tribe, and even race. Access is easy, and the creativity of native artists and musicians finds fertile ground in the music and regalia.

Powwows also offer safe, sober environments that bring communities together and usually involve people of all ages, making them a healthy social option. Some tribal members feel that the financial support given to powwows is excessive and eclipses expenditures on other even more important initiatives such as tribal language and culture revitalization. As money motivates participation, some see powwows as part of the rapid cultural change engulfing Indian country. Even though powwow is positive by itself, many say it is not and could never be a substitute for older lifeways and customs.

Northern Wind Singers at Leech Lake Contest Powwow in Cass Lake, Minnesota, September 2009

What do the different styles of dance mean?

There are many different styles of dance. The "men's traditional" style, which typically includes a feather bustle worn on the back and a feathered roach, dog soldier hat, or headdress, is one of the oldest and one of the most common. It is an evolution of older war regalia, where warriors earned feathers in battle and displayed them at war and scalp dances (but not always in battle). Today, it is not expected that those who wear such regalia have "earned" their feathers, although the feathers are still highly respected. Because in former times each feather represented a human being who was killed or wounded, a feather that is acci-

dentally dropped in the powwow arena is usually picked up only
by military veterans, who use a special song to dance around it
and retrieve the fallen "comrade." Traditional dancers mimic the
actions of warriors and hunters scouting for enemies or game.

Another common men's dance is the "grass dance." Originally
a distinct style used only in the Omaha Grass Dance Society, it
spread to other tribes and became very popular in the 1970s and
remains so today. Dancers do not usually have feather bustles,
although they do often have head roaches made of porcupine

Men's traditional dancer

and deer hair, sometimes with a feather or two. The body of the outfit includes aprons with long fringe that mimics the action of grass blowing in the wind. The dancers themselves spin, turn, and move their feet as if they were moving in tall grass, all to the beat of the drum.

Men's "fancy dance" is a derivation of the older traditional style. It incorporates many elements of traditional regalia, but usually with bright colors and double bustles that are not always made of eagle feathers. The dancers display rapid footwork and even gymnastic moves, spinning, cartwheeling, and jumping. Among the most popular styles to watch, it is much more widely practiced at competition powwows than traditional ones.

There are other styles of men's dance as well, most of which involve mimicking the actions or motions of birds or animals. There are also many variations in styles of beadwork. The eastern Great Lakes often use more floral designs, while the western Great Lakes and Plains tribes often favor more geometric patterns, but dancers are free to create whatever they wish. Although some purchase their dance regalia, most make their own or have family members help them, incorporating personal colors acquired at their naming ceremonies, from dreams, or while fasting.

In older dance forms that predated powwows, women did not always dance or sing in all tribes. Today, women sing on powwow drums in Washington State and other places but are often forbidden or strongly discouraged from doing so in other parts of Indian country. The same is no longer true for dance. Powwow dancing is as popular and widely practiced among women as it is among men.

The "women's traditional" dance has many variations in regalia. Southern Plains style often incorporate elk teeth as evidence of the hunting skill of a woman's mate. Western tribes sometimes make use of the cowry shell, although that item has religious significance for many Great Lakes tribes and is less common there. Typically, the outfits incorporate elaborate beadwork and very long fringe, and gentle dance motions rock the

Men's grass dancer

Men's fancy dancer

Women's traditional dancer

Women's jingle dress dancer

Opposite:
Women's fancy shawl dancer

fringe back and forth. Often, women's traditional dancers ring the outside edge of the dance arbor in a circle around the men.

The women's "jingle dress" style involves a long, tight dress covered in numerous jingles, often constructed from snuff can lids or other metal. The jingles make a swooshing sound. The jingle dress style evolved from an Ojibwe man's dream of the dress around the time of World War I. The jingle part of the regalia was believed to have healing power. Sometimes jingle dress healing songs are performed at powwows, but usually the secular version of the dance is on display.

Women's "fancy shawl" is the other popular form of female dance. The attire involves a colorful dress and shawl. The dancer spins and moves her arms to mimic the actions of a butterfly coming out of its cocoon and flitting about the arena.

Why are "49" songs sung in English?

The "49" song accompanies one of the few partner dances exhibited at powwows. The music is differentiated from other powwow songs by its slower and syncopated rhythm, to which partners hold hands and move in a long line, twisting and winding around the arena, following the moves of the lead couple. The music uses English in part because this dance is inspired by French and English partner dance customs but also because is it an especially popular form of music among young singers. Over time, it has sought to entertain with wit and even popular culture lines, such as "you got the right one, baby," and "good ol' fashioned Indian lovin.'" It's part of the culture of the music.

How come they have a prize purse at powwows?

Not all Indians are happy about this development, although it is a huge part of the life of many native people. Competition for prize money in various styles of dance and singing derives from the rodeo component of powwow's origins. As the dances became more rigidly stylized and secular and less ceremonial, this was an easy segue. Today, tribes with significant financial means often offer large prize purses to draw numerous singers, dancers, and spectators. It is seen as a way to show local hospitality, raise the profile of the host community in Indian country, and demonstrate authentic culture to outsiders.

Some Indians oppose the proliferation of contest powwows over traditional powwows and other cultural forms. They say that placing a monetary value on participants' abilities to sing and dance supplants older cultural ideals of community cohesion, inclusiveness, and respectful generosity.

Powwow is the largest and fastest-growing part of Indian culture today. It is everywhere. Tribes like Leech Lake (Minnesota) spend over a hundred thousand dollars on prize money for Labor Day contest powwows alone; and Leech Lake has at least a dozen powwows a year, ranging in size from its large contest powwow to several smaller community powwows. The powwow budget for Leech Lake completely eclipses tribal expenditures on traditional culture and Ojibwe language revitalization, and that's what really bothers some tribal members.

Tribes and tribal people are agents of their own cultural change. The modern powwow is a welcome, healthy gathering of people from many communities. It is a joyous social event and source of community pride. But it is not a substitution for traditional religion or ways of life.

Can white people dance at powwows?

Yes. Although there are prohibitions against the participation of outsiders in ceremonial events and customs for some tribes, powwow has no such official barriers. Furthermore, as the number of Indians with light complexions has grown over the past few decades, many nonnative people may even be assumed to be native at powwows. The powwow emcee will announce to the audience if there is a special honor song or exhibition song for a certain style of dance. Otherwise, powwow music is considered and often called inter-tribal—open to people of all tribes and races.

Schemitzun Powwow poster, Mashantucket Pequot, 1995

Do women sing at powwows?

Yes. Women from all tribes sing in a variety of secular and ceremonial functions, but there are rules and sometimes those rules are gendered. Some types of ceremonial music are exclusively male and other types exclusively female. For most Great Lakes tribes and many others, women do not touch ceremonial big drums or even powwow drums. Men sit around those drums and do the drumming and most of the singing, although women can and often do stand or sit behind the men, singing with them, usually an octave above to the same melody.

The first ceremonial drum that the Dakota gave to the Ojibwe came through the vision of a Dakota woman who "saw" men singing at the drum and women sitting behind the men, singing with them. That practice carried over to secular forms of singing on large drums for the Ojibwe, Menominee, Potawatomi, and others. For those tribes, it is not seen as an exclusion of women but rather as the greatest way to respect the vision of the woman who "gave birth to the drum." Tribes in the Pacific Northwest do not have the same prohibitions, and women often sing on larger powwow drums there. But tribal people respect the traditions of the host communities, including their varying protocols for gender and singing.

What is the protocol for gifts at powwows?

Visitors are not required to give gifts at powwows, where it is the host community's responsibility to show generosity to others. Toward the end of the powwow, the host community usually sponsors a giveaway, during which they make large piles of blankets and other goods and distribute them to dancers, helpers, and spectators. Sometimes a family will sponsor a giveaway. Once in a while, a family that is having a hard time might ask for a blanket dance to solicit donations for travel or health care. Contributing money during a blanket dance is a free will donation.

Tribal Languages

"This is our language. It is the sound
of the waves crashing on the shore, the
sound of the wind in the pines, the rustle
of the leaves in autumn. It is the sound
of the birds singing in the forest and the
wolves howling in the distance. This is
our language, from which we obtain life,
our means of knowing who we are, this
sacred gift, bestowed upon us by our creator."

GORDON JOURDAIN, Lac La Croix (Ontario)[1]

How many tribal languages are spoken in North America?

There may have been as many as five hundred distinct tribal languages in North America prior to sustained contact with Europeans. There are now around 180, but the number is shrinking quickly. All world languages are members of families, such as the Germanic or Romance language families. And languages in the same families (like English and German) have some similarities, although they are not always mutually intelligible. There are fifty-six language families in North America and over three times that number in South America. Sometimes Native American languages spoken by groups that are geographically adjacent (like Ojibwe and Dakota) are as different as Chinese and English.

Which ones have a chance to be here a hundred years from now?

There are currently about twenty tribal languages in the United States and Canada spoken by significant numbers of children. They include Ojibwe, Cree, Ottawa, Diné (Navajo), Hawaiian, Tiwa and Tewa (Pueblo), Hopi, Apsáalooke (Crow), Mohawk, and Lakota. But even most of these tribes do not have any monolingual speakers of the tribal language. Usually, English is used for some aspects of daily life (school, job, or social). Even in remote parts of the Navajo Reservation (Arizona), Ni'ihau (Hawaii), or Lac La Croix First Nation (Ontario), where there are enclaves that have 100 percent fluency in the tribal language, mainstream media is coming in via satellite dish and English is starting to become the peer language for some of the youngest age groups. People are worried about the future vitality of tribal languages everywhere in the United States and Canada. In Mexico, some of the thirty Mayan languages have large numbers of speakers (six million total), including significant groups of monolingual speakers, and their future seems certain in some places.

Why are fluency rates higher in Canada?

They aren't that much higher. Like indigenous communities throughout the Americas, most Canadian First Nations are in language crisis. The missionary activity started early in the colonial experience there, although the residential boarding school system started (and ended) later than in the United States. That timeline, coupled with the geographic isolation of some communities (accessed primarily by floatplane or boat), has helped to keep rates higher in a few areas.

Some communities also have unique circumstances. Manitoulin Island (in the Georgian Bay of Lake Huron) has a large tract of unceded Indian land that provided a higher degree of geographic isolation and thus mitigated some of the language pressure seen in other parts of Ontario. Another example is a large group of Dakota who escaped military attack and persecution in southern Minnesota in 1862 by settling in Canada. Their descendents have been especially tenacious about language revitalization in recent years, creating a living resource for today's Minnesota Dakota communities in their own language revitalization work.

It seems like tribal languages won't give native people a leg up in the modern world. Why are tribal languages important to Indians?

In fact, tribal languages do give Indians a leg up in the modern world. The Waadookodaading Ojibwe Immersion Charter School in Reserve, Wisconsin, has for ten years garnered a 100 percent pass rate on state-mandated tests administered in English, and the teachers do not speak to the kids in English until the higher grades. Even wealthy, predominantly white suburban school districts don't usually score so consistently high. Tribal language education is a powerful tool for the development of everything from cognitive function to basic self-esteem.

Indian people value their languages for many other reasons as well. They are cornerstones of identity, and their use keeps us recognizable to our ancestors. They are defining features of nationhood. The retention of tribal languages tells the world that we have not been assimilated, in spite of five hundred years of concerted effort to achieve that. They are the only customary languages for many ceremonies, a gateway to spiritual understanding. And tribal languages encapsulate unique tribal world views. They define us as distinct peoples.

Why should tribal languages be important to everyone else?

I always tell the deans and president at Bemidji State University, where I work, that when people call for the "Department of Foreign Languages" to be sure to direct them to the English

Department. Tribal languages are modern, domestic languages. They are the first languages of this land and the first languages of the first Americans. These facts alone should make their retention especially important. The proven links between academic achievement and cultural and linguistic competency for native youth also indicate that everyone should want the most successful strategies employed to bridge the educational and economic achievement gaps for Indians so that natives can be the best possible neighbors and need fewer entitlements to alleviate poverty, reducing the tax burden for all. But even more important, the survival of tribal languages and cultures is a litmus test for the morality of our nation and its ability to provide for the needs of all of its citizens. If the United States can enable and support the retention of cultural and linguistic diversity, its strength and moral position is obvious, rather than tainted.

What are the challenges to successfully revitalizing tribal languages?

Some tribal languages have no speakers left and very few written resources. The Hebrew language was revived almost two thousand years after it became moribund, but in a form highly altered from its original use and with the help of lots of written material and a large population of people committed to seeing that result. The deck is stacked against many tribes accomplishing something similar. The places that have a good chance of making a successful intervention have a critical mass of fluent speakers and a growing body of resources (books, audio recordings, and computer materials for instruction). The challenges are finding adequate language resources, certified teachers fluent in the target language, and financial support. Often tribal government support is limited, as resources are diverted to entitlements or because tribal leaders do not see the value of preserving their own languages. Lighting the fire for a major revitalization is challenging in many places, even where the potential for intervention is great.

When were tribal languages first written down?

Some tribes did write before European contact. The Mayans had a unique system of writing. The Ojibwe used mnemonic devices written on birch bark to preserve critical information. But the formal writing systems developed for most tribal languages were introduced after European contact. Missionaries wanted the Bible and other religious texts to enter the minds and hearts of Indians as quickly as possible, and some did a lot of work with tribal languages to achieve their goal. Most systems used roman letters. Some, like syllabics (employed for Cree and Ojibwe), used unique symbols. Sequoyah, a Cherokee silversmith, developed a syllabary for Cherokee. His syllabary—the first to be independently created by a member of a nonliterate people—was formally adopted by the Cherokee Nation in 1825 and is still employed today, recently being incorporated as a language on the Macintosh and iPhone operating systems.

Sequoyah developed the Cherokee syllabary even though he was not literate in other languages.

Many tribal languages were never written. Why do they write them now?

At one point in time, white people never used cars, so why do they use them now? Because it makes life easier and more efficient. Indians also at one point did not have cars, or electricity, or writing systems for most of their languages. But those things can improve quality of life or ease of communication. Still, there is not universal agreement about the writing of tribal language. The Pueblos are among the strictest in their insistence that the language remain oral and not written. Most tribes accept the writing of tribal languages but may not agree on specific writing systems. In most places, there is an increasing awareness that writing can be a critical part of developing needed resources, preserving critical information, and stabilizing languages.

Why is it funnier in Indian?

All languages have their words comprised of smaller parts of words called *morphemes*. In English, those morphemes come from the language's Germanic roots, from Latin, Greek, and many other languages, so everyday speakers of English do not commonly know the roots of words. But the opposite is often true for many tribal languages, whose speakers know the deeper meanings behind their words and can then communicate on two levels—using words and the deeper meaning behind them. That makes it easier to have plays on words, puns, descriptions, and names converge in ways that give greater meaning and humor to many situations.

In Ojibwe, for example, the word *giboodiyegwaazonag* means "pants" or, literally, "leggings that sew up the hind end." Ojibwe people must have thought pants were hilariously impractical in a cold-weather climate where one had to take the entire works down to relieve oneself, when someone with a skirt or breechclout and leggings had quick and easy access. Even today, when

Ojibwe people regularly wear pants instead of breechclouts, the word still elicits a chuckle.

How do tribal languages encapsulate a different world view?

Just as morphemes carry possibilities for humor, they also carry deeper and more resonant meanings that shape attitudes. In Ojibwe, for example, the word for an old woman, *mindimooye*, literally means "one who holds things together," describing the role of the family matriarch. In English, *old woman, elderly woman*, and *aged woman* all speak to age rather than to a more exalted function for elder women in society. Many women dye their hair, get Botox injections or face lifts, and rarely admit to their true age in order to combat the appearance of growing older, because the world view of many English language speakers devalues the role and appearance of older women. But in the Ojibwe language, there is a revered place for elder women, one reflected in core values, actions, and the language itself. You don't have to tell Ojibwe speakers to respect their elders. The respect is built right in with every word one would use to refer to them. Even the gender-neutral term for elder in Ojibwe, *gichi-aya'aa*, literally means "great being."

Politics

> "What we now call an Indian nation was
> a modern invention born at the moment
> of treaty."
>
> SCOTT LYONS, *X-Marks: Native Signatures of Assent*

What is sovereignty?

Sovereignty means supreme and independent authority over a geographic area. Indian nations are sovereign because they have such power and control over reservations. Tribal sovereignty is the basis for most fundamentally different legal and political conditions in Indian country. Treaty rights, casinos, and different tax laws are only possible in Indian country because tribes are sovereign. That sovereignty often enables tribes to protect tribal languages, cultures, and land in ways that would be completely impossible if it did not exist.

Sovereignty is what makes a tribe different from a cultural enclave like the Amish. The Amish have preserved distinct cultural traditions and languages, but they are still subject to federal and state laws. The Meskwaki Nation (Iowa) and other tribes have preserved distinct cultural traditions and language but are not subject to all state and federal laws. Thus, the Meskwaki exercise independent control over their reservation and make their own laws about gaming and taxation. They are sovereign.

Tribal sovereignty is a powerful political authority, but it is not absolute. There are some limitations to scope and depth of tribal sovereignty. Over many decades, the U.S. and Canadian governments have sought to erode the political power of tribes and diminish their sovereignty with some, but not complete, success. Indians nations do not maintain their own armies, for example. The U.S. and Canadian federal governments have significant power over some aspects of tribal life and law. Specific dimensions of tribal sovereignty, including treaty rights, gaming, criminal law, and taxation, are detailed throughout the rest of this book.

Why do Indians have reservations?

Indians used to own all of North and South America. Reservations are not gifts to Indians from the U.S. government: they are retained portions of the original tribal homelands—the parts that were not sold or taken. When tribes made treaties with the U.S. government in which they sold much of their land, those treaties affirmed the special status of the retained, reserved lands and that of tribes as independent governments—another major difference between Indians and other racial or ethnic groups in the United States.

Starting in the 1830s, a series of court cases often called the Marshall Trilogy (after Chief Justice John Marshall, who wrote the opinions for the court) further affirmed the special status of tribal government and reservation land and made it clear that state governments did not have jurisdiction on reservations or over Indian people. Reservations are nations, not just cultural enclaves, landholdings, or communities. Some limitations were later put on tribal nationhood through acts of Congress, but the basic reason for the existence of Indian reservations remains the same.

Why isn't being American enough? Why do Indians need reservations today?

Reservations are home to around half of the enrolled Indian population in America, and like most Americans, Indians love their home. The connection that Indians have to their reservations is especially strong. In many places, numerous generations of family members are buried in the same ground. Nobody wants to give that up. And there are sacred places and ceremony sites on reservations that serve as the center for spiritual work that still sustains many tribal people.

But the preservation of reservations is about more than special places and ancient histories. The continuation of tribal government is a continuation of tribal self-rule (in spite of some limitations). Many Indians feel that their ancestors paid very dearly—and they themselves are still paying dearly—for the right to have their reserved lands and tribal governments. Reservations are nations in the eyes of many Indians, and they carry powerful patriotism for those nations. It is true that there are plenty of problems on reservations, ranging from poverty to pervasive substance abuse in some places. Quite a few reservations have unemployment rates over 50 percent and most have unemployment rates over 20 percent. Reservation governments are trying to remedy their problems through education programs and employment opportunities. The federal government has been unwilling to make a major intervention on the issue of Indian poverty. Tribal members see the greatest hope for addressing these and other problems in Indian country in the programs of their tribal governments.

In a somewhat surprising counter to these aspects of reservations, there is a common misconception that reservations are nothing more than concentration camps. Some people even think there may be barbed wire or other physical obstacles to the free travel of Native Americans. That view is just plain untrue.

In addition to all the reasons that Indians love their homelands and need their tribal governments, many draw attention to the fact that the federal government promised to reserve those lands and tribal governments in perpetuity as partial payment for the balance of the land obtained in treaties. If the United States reneges on that promise, its own integrity is compromised and the cultural and economic well-being of the tribal population would suffer.

Why do Indians have treaty rights? What other rights do they have that differ from most people?

There are two primary reasons why Indians have certain rights that other Americans do not. The first has to do with treaties. When the U.S. federal government wanted land from Indians, negotiators had to pay Indians or promise Indians different things in order to obtain the land from them. Tribal leaders had a different concept of land ownership than that held by Europeans. When they advocated for their people, the main thing they insisted upon was the right to hunt, fish, gather, and travel on all of their lands, including soon-to-be-ceded lands. Often, the U.S. government obtained title to Indian land but agreed to allow Indian people to retain their right to use the land, even the land that was just sold. These rights, often referred to as *usufructuary rights,* are the basis of the treaty rights that many Native Americans enjoy today. They explain why hunting seasons and methods may vary and be more liberal for Indians on Indian land than they are for others governed exclusively by state laws and why tribal rights sometimes extend outside reservation boundaries. It is part of the payment the U.S. government made for the land.

The other major reason Indians have different rights is that state governments have no authority over reservations or tribal governments except for individual criminal cases, and that is only in the places where Public Law 280 (see page 104) is in effect. In the U.S. constitution, all rights not specifically granted to the federal government were reserved by the states. As a result, most of the basic regulations and civil laws that Americans deal with on a day-to-day basis come from state government rather than the federal government. Enrolled members living on reservations fall under a different jurisdictional framework.

Left: Tribal fisherman Vincent Wolfe at North Twin Lake (Wisconsin), 1990, waiting by barricades erected by police to protect Ojibwe tribal members exercising treaty rights

Below: Leech Lake (Minnesota) band member Elias Treuer harvesting wild rice, September 2011

What is allotment?

Allotment is the practice of taking tribal land, which was held in trust for the common use of all tribal members, and splitting it into parcels to be owned by each tribal member, with the remaining land sold to settlers and private companies. The profits from the land sales were then to be used by the Department of the Interior to fund assimilation programs for American Indian people. The Dawes Act enabled this policy on tribal land in the United States in 1887. Of the 155 million acres of land held in trust for Indians on reservations, 50 million were allotted to tribal members, usually in 160-acre parcels. The remaining 105 million acres of land were deemed "surplus" and opened for white settlement.

It would have been better for Indians to allot all tribal land to Indians or to avoid allotment altogether. One of the reasons the government created the policy was to open reservations to timber, mineral, and land speculators and settlers. Land allotted to Indians quickly flew out of their hands as well. In spite of trust period protections, in which Indians were not supposed to be able to sell their allotments for twenty-five years, numerous Indians fell victim to land speculators. Over the course of the policy from 1887 to 1933, the federal government passed many amendments to the legislation in order to limit trust protections and to make the sale of Indian parcels easier. As a result of this policy, Indians retain less than 10 percent of their own reservations in many places.

A few reservations were able to avoid allotment, including Red Lake (Minnesota) and Menominee (Wisconsin). Usually, the success of communities in avoiding allotment had less to do with a kind American government than it did with their relative geographic isolation or other political considerations. In Red Lake, for example, the government asked for allotment, a major land cession, and relocation all at the same time. They got the land cession but not allotment or relocation. Even today, all land at Red Lake is held in trust for all tribal members, and the main reservation has never endured allotment. Red Lake and the few other tribes that avoided the policy are the exception rather than the rule, however: allotment was the means by which two-thirds of the reservation tribal land base was lost.

Why does my land have clouded title?

Most reservations in the United States comprise both tribal land and land that is owned by private citizens. On many of those reservations, nonnative people own most of the private land. A fair number of those people have titles to that land that are "clouded." *Clouded title* means that proof of rightful ownership is not clear, usually due to illegal or fraudulent actions in the past. Multiple parties claim a right to the title of clouded parcels.

Between 1784 and 1871, the U.S. government signed 370 treaties with American Indian people to obtain 720 cessions of land. The lands remaining in tribal hands were subject to a lot of land fraud, lease fraud, and mineral lease fraud, especially during the allotment era (1887–1933). Simply put, there were resources on reservations that outsiders wanted. Those who wanted the resources did not always have great respect for the rightful Indian owners of the land. Joseph Auginaush, an elder from the White Earth Reservation, showed me a $24 grocery receipt, explaining that the grocery clerk from Roy Lake went to the allotment officer at White Earth and demanded the Auginaush family allotment in lieu of payment for the family's grocery bill, by which he obtained exclusive title to their 160-acre allotment. The grocer sold the allotment, but the people he sold it to now had land with "clouded title." The Auginaush family was never compensated for the theft, even though they had no court hearing or formal notice of the land transactions. Theirs was a typical case.

After generations of ownership by nonnative people and multiple sales of those parcels of land, nonnative families who did not commit fraud and have lived on reservations for generations now cannot obtain clear title to their own land and have lower property values and undergo cumbersome procedures to sell or bequeath land. Many Indians were ripped off, and their descendants have been unable to access the land they should have received as a birthright.

A law that declared all current owners as the rightful owners of land on reservations would simply legalize the theft of many of those parcels from Indians. This solution would be neither morally nor legally right in this country, which has valued property rights above most others. But a law that granted land parcels to the descendants of the original owners would disregard the rights of inheritance and ownership of many nonnative families. Thus, resolutions have been elusive, and many parcels of land on reservations continue to have clouded title.

Is something being done about clouded title?

There have been attempts to clarify clouded title on Indian reservations. By 1946, when the U.S. government established the Indian Claims Commission, tribes had already filed 219 land claims cases in the U.S. Court of Claims. The commission of three judges settled 285 cases but was authorized to offer only monetary compensation for land lost via fraud. However, many tribes preferred land return to monetary compensation, and the commission did not solve all land conflicts. In 1978, the federal government passed legislation ending the ICC and sent the remaining 170 undecided cases to the U.S. Court of Claims. The Oneida and Lakota cases are among the most famous of these. The Lakota refused their large court-ordered settlement, insisting upon the return of ancestral lands. The Oneida encountered many complications because of relocation from New York to Wisconsin and because of state interference in the federal-tribal relationship; their case has yet to be resolved.[1]

Another ongoing legal action that seeks to quantify land fraud and make reparations for it as a means to secure unclouded title to current owners is in the *Cobell v. Salazar* land claims settlement. The Cobell settlement is a source of great contention in Indian country today. This settlement focuses primarily on trust funds and trust lands, most of which originated under allotment policy. Native Americans who are enrolled members and can prove fraud on parcels of land or funds that the U.S. government administered on their behalf can work through an incredibly long and enormously cumbersome process to receive partial compensation. Many Native Americans feel that when all is said and done, most Indians will receive, at most, meager compensation, but their right to contest outsiders' illegitimate title to reservation land will be forever sacrificed.

If tribes had hereditary chiefs, how come there is a democratic process in place for selecting tribal leaders in most places today?

From the genesis of the U.S. government until 1934, its representatives systematically deposed existing tribal leaders and dismantled leadership structures, moved Indian people onto reservations—often concentrating many chiefs and their constituents in one place—and then put nonnative Indian agents in charge of tribal affairs. In 1934, the Indian Reorganization Act shifted the U.S. bureaucracy that dealt with Indians (the Office of Indian Affairs, soon to be renamed the Bureau of Indian Affairs) from a supervisory agency to an advisory agency.

It was a major policy change, but it still took decades for tribal people to organize modern governments. When they did, there was a lot of variation, from more traditional leadership structures to (more commonly) democratic forms. The U.S. government provided draft constitutions to tribes, but those drafts were highly flawed, based on a corporate governance model rather than a political one with checks and balances. Tribes are still (with varying degrees of success) seeking to remedy those draft constitutions and remake tribal government in their own ways. The Indian Self-Determination and Education Assistance Act of 1975 enabled the U.S. secretaries of the interior, health, education, and welfare to contract with and make grants directly to tribes, which served to further strengthen tribal powers.

What's the Indian Reorganization Act?

The Indian Reorganization Act (IRA), passed in 1934, is the piece of legislation that changed the role of the Office of Indian Affairs (soon to be renamed the Bureau of Indian Affairs) from a supervisory agency that managed every major facet of Indian government (without tribal input or representation) to an advisory one. In a short time, tribes developed modern tribal governments much as they are today, and the era of Indian self-determination began. Tribes could once again have greater say in designing their own futures. The IRA also ended allotment and returned remaining tribal lands to federal trust, which helped stabilize the tribal land base.

The IRA was welcomed by many tribes, but it came with its own problems: the U.S. Department of the Interior retained substantial power over tribal affairs, tribal citizens had few rights or protections, and the new government structures that emerged after the IRA did not usually reflect traditional tribal governance structures or values (see page 94). In some cases, the IRA also merged previously autonomous Indian nations into one tribal government. For example, Sandy Lake (Minnesota) was established as an independent reservation in 1855 and had always had its own chiefs and independent political structure, but after the IRA it was folded into the Mille Lacs Reservation, where it had a district representative but no longer functioned independently, making Sandy Lake a smaller part of a larger Indian political structure. Many people from that community still feel betrayed, isolated, and disempowered by the change.

What are the Minnesota Chippewa Tribe and the Great Lakes Inter-Tribal Council?

Each tribe in the United States is its own sovereign entity—a native nation. They independently make their own decisions, subject only to the Major Crimes Act, Public Law 280, and other federal limitations on tribal sovereignty. However, in some places, those native nations have pooled their political and economic resources to work cooperatively. Sometimes the connections between tribes in these types of arrangements are constitutionally stipulated, meaning the member tribes, the overarching agency (Minnesota Chippewa Tribe, for example), and the Bureau of Indian Affairs all have political interactions with the tribal citizenship process and other critical dimensions of tribal sovereignty.

The Minnesota Chippewa Tribe (MCT) is comprised of six Ojibwe nations in Minnesota, each with its own reservation. They have much in common: language, culture, history, and treaties, some of which were signed by leaders from most of the member reservations. In fact, the Nelson Act of 1889, which implemented allotment for most Ojibwe in Minnesota and addressed other land issues for them, created some of the impetus for creating the MCT. Several independent Ojibwe nations shared interest in tracts of land and compensation from the sale of that land, which was officially held "in common" for all of them. When modern tribal governments were created after the 1934 Indian Reorganization Act, establishing the MCT two years later seemed like the easiest way to deal with the land and money issues for the member tribes in the future. The MCT administered trust lands for member tribes for a long time, but over the past twenty years Leech Lake and other tribes have been slowly asserting greater control over trust land and tribal leases of it.

The MCT was designed to enable cooperative work and greater political clout. But it has had other effects as well. One of the reservations, White Earth, comprises one-third of the MCT's tribal population (and one-third of many revenue streams). White Earth has often been stymied in its efforts to pass major meaningful constitutional reforms because the other member reservations do not agree with the proposed changes to tribal citizenship and do not want to release White Earth from the MCT because of the financial repercussions.

The Great Lakes Inter-Tribal Council has membership from

twelve different reservations in Wisconsin, some of which have very different tribal heritage, languages, and cultural practices. The conceptual framework for the Great Lakes Inter-Tribal Council is to empower all member reservations politically and financially. The GLITC has nothing to do with the MCT, but some of the benefits and problems of the organizational structures are similar.

Why do so many Indians live in urban areas today? What is relocation?

Some reservations have unemployment rates over 50 percent. Anyone who lives in a place with limited opportunities for financial betterment or even basic survival seeks a way out. That's how America filled up with immigrants, and it's part of the explanation for how so many Indians left reservations. It's also true that Indians have a high rate of marriage to people of different races, which helps bring a lot of Indians off-reservation.

Also, some reservations like Leech Lake (Minnesota) own less than 4 percent of their land due to policies like allotment (see page 91). Even enrolled members have a hard time finding housing, and people are forced to look elsewhere. Enrollment criteria for reservations are a major source of contention as well: there are now more than twice as many Indians self-identifying for the census than there are enrolled members (tribal citizens). The non-enrolled Indians are not eligible for tribal housing and other programs.

In addition to all of these variables, the U.S. government made it official policy to relocate Indians from reservations to urban areas in the 1950s. The government appropriated funds to provide tribal members with one-way transportation and rental assistance for the first month. Thousands of Indians took advantage of the program, believing they would find greater financial opportunities in cities. Milwaukee, Minneapolis, Chicago, Denver, and Oakland developed large Indian populations as a result of this policy. But relocations failed to deliver the financial betterment promised. There was still a racial barrier to gainful employment for people of color in the 1950s and 1960s, and Indians who moved under the policy were soon even more impoverished than their reservation counterparts. Still, the establishment of substantial urban Indian populations was a permanent change.

The U.S. government circulated brochures to Indians to entice them to move to urban areas as part of relocation initiatives in the 1950s.

What is termination?

The U.S. government did a lot of experimenting with Indian policy. Although the Indian Reorganization Act (1934; see page 95) had opened the self-determination era, only two decades later the government was looking for ways to diminish tribal sovereignty and terminate it altogether, which is exactly what this policy was all about. The government compiled a list of tribes from the most "acculturated" to the least, with plans to terminate their political existence in that order. They didn't see termination as a punishment but rather as the culmination of years of successful assimilation programs.

As the government proceeded to terminate the sovereign status of tribes one at a time, it quickly became evident that the policy was a disaster. The Menominee, who had pioneered the world's first sustainable forest harvesting program and banked $10 million with no help from the U.S. government, had to shut down the operation. Without legal standing as a sovereign nation, Menominee land and business operations became taxable, they lost their management team, and then they started to lose the very land on which they harvested trees. The revenue stream diminished and then disappeared. Tribal members had no jobs. The new Menominee "corporation" that owned the former reservation lands had to sell the land to pay the taxes on the remaining land. Tribal member Ada Deer said, "It was like burning your house down to stay warm in the winter."[2] The federal government had to spend more in welfare payments to tribal members than it had cost to support the Menominee tribal government, and Menominee County became the poorest in the state of Wisconsin.

After years of sustained protest, the terminated Menominee were reinstated, as were some other tribes in the 1970s and 1980s, such as the Klamath, Coquille, and Catawba. Most of the other 109 terminated tribes were never reinstated.[3] Many continue to struggle to gain a return of status. Any trust tribes and tribal members had for the federal government was shattered once again.

Why do Indians have their own police and courts in some places?

The right of tribes to maintain their own police and court systems is inherent, even though the court system and government have often tried to recast and diminish the nature of tribal sovereignty. Unless a treaty or act of Congress limits tribal sovereignty (see page 86), it is unhindered. For this reason, tribes have different laws about gaming and gambling, hunting and fishing, and many other things. Despite the fact that the right of tribes to build their own police and courts is inherent, some have not exercised that right. The U.S. government controlled reservations for decades and systematically dismantled tribal leadership structures in most places. Only since 1934 have tribes been able to assume greater control over their own governments.

Building courts and successfully managing police forces takes a tremendous amount of logistical support and money. Al-

Indian police force, White Earth Reservation, Minnesota, 1908

though federal appropriations and grants can augment a tribe's efforts to build police and court systems, government support is never enough, and most tribal court and police administrations have to do a lot of external fund-raising. It takes time to develop qualified police officers, lawyers, and judges. Tribes are reluctant to spend the resources needed to develop a court if they can only hire outsiders. Therefore, tribes with small populations or limited financial resources have been somewhat less likely than larger tribes to develop police and court systems, although there are exceptions. The federal government has passed laws like Public Law 280 (see page 104), which further eroded the jurisdiction of tribal governments for some states, but those laws are complex and not in place on all reservations.

Why does the FBI investigate murders on some reservations?

Most lawyers do not understand Indian law and jurisdiction very well, and most citizens understand even less. Tribal leaders used to have exclusive say about matters of justice in their communities. Over a period of many decades, the U.S. government systematically attacked and eroded the authority of tribal leaders.

One of the first major legal intrusions into tribal sovereignty came in the late 1800s in response to a decision from the U.S. Supreme Court in the case of *Ex Parte Crow Dog*. A Lakota man named Crow Dog killed another Lakota named Spotted Tail in 1881. Tribal leaders convened a traditional tribal council and decided that Crow Dog would have to make financial reparations to Spotted Tail's widow and provide for her well-being for the rest of his life and furthermore exiled him and his entire family for four generations. (Leonard Crow Dog, a well-known spiritual leader for the American Indian Movement, is the last of the four generations to live in exile from the main community at Rosebud.) Spotted Tail, who had been acknowledged as a chief by General George Cook in 1876, had cooperated with the U.S. government rather than resisting. Many nonnative officials felt that Crow Dog was getting away with "the red man's revenge." They arrested him, tried him for murder, and sentenced him to hang.

Crow Dog obtained a lawyer and fought his case all the way to the Supreme Court, where he won a major decision. The court ruled that the Lakota could not be subject to the jurisdiction of a federal, state, or territorial court and that the ability of tribes to address such offenses was an attribute of tribal sovereignty that had not been specifically ended by an act of Congress. Neither the states nor the federal government had the power to hang Crow Dog. There was a public outcry in the United States about Indians getting away with murder; many lawmakers used that sentiment to develop a new policy approach that would strengthen the U.S. government's power over Indians on tribal land.

The Major Crimes Act (1885) gave the U.S. government jurisdiction over major crimes between Indians on Indian land. From 1885 on, federal authorities investigated Indian-on-Indian crimes in cases of murder, rape, arson, manslaughter, burglary, larceny, and assault with deadly intent. Initially, this was done through auspices of the Indian agent on each reservation. Courts of Indian Offenses, administered by the U.S. government, were the venue through which justice was administered to Indians. Eventually, as the Office of Indian Affairs became advisory rather than supervisory, the FBI assumed the role of primary investigator for Indian-on-Indian crimes on Indian land. The Major Crimes Act was amended many times, and the list of offenses expanded significantly.

All of this was complicated enough, but the U.S. federal government later passed legislation that sought to give some state governments authority over criminal affairs in Indian country. Public Law 280 further complicated the arena of jurisdiction in Indian country. Essentially, the U.S. federal government has authority over major crimes everywhere in Indian country unless Public Law 280 has specifically granted that jurisdiction to state governments. A detailed discussion of Public Law 280 appears below (page 104).

Crow Dog's landmark case affirmed tribal sovereignty but also convinced the U.S. government to pass the Major Crimes Act and assert federal jurisdiction over major crimes on Indian land.

Murder is not a federal crime in America. Each state government has declared murder to be illegal and devises its own statutes on crime. Because each state maintains its own jurisdiction, some states have the death penalty while others do not. Indian law is the only significant exception to state jurisdiction over capital crimes. Among other things, sentencing guidelines tend to be stricter at the federal level, meaning that Indians in many states endure harsher punishment than do their white neighbors who commit the same crimes.

Why do state law enforcement agencies investigate murders on some reservations? What is Public Law 280?

In 1953, Public Law 280 was passed, and it has had a substantial and long-lasting impact on many tribes.[4] This federal congressional act only applied to tribes in five states—Oregon, Nebraska, California, Wisconsin, and Minnesota. Eleven other states were later added to the list. Many states declined the jurisdiction when it was offered to them because it would require them to provide services to tribal members that the federal government had previously funded.

Until passage of Public Law 280, tribes had authority over their own reservations, free from all but U.S. federal interference. The federal government had controlled reservation courts and government before the Indian Reorganization Act in 1934 (see page 95) and assumed an advisory role after that. Major crimes remained under federal jurisdiction since passage of the Major Crimes Act in 1885. With Public Law 280, states specifically named in the law would assume all criminal and limited civil jurisdiction over Indians. The complex web of state criminal law now formally applied to Indians in several states for the first time in history.

A few exceptions to Public Law 280 exist, even in states where it was applied. Red Lake Tribal Chairman Roger Jourdain (Minnesota) was an exceptionally shrewd and savvy leader who constantly scrutinized every legislative agenda and U.S. government action. Jourdain immediately recognized Public Law 280 as an intrusion into Red Lake's sovereignty, intervened before the bill was introduced to Congress, and successfully fought to have Red Lake exempted from the law. Tribes facing impending termination like the Menominee were also exempted.

In the 1950s, tribal governments were new, weak, and unaware of Public Law 280's implications, so the law passed without the consent of or consultation with other tribal leaders in affected communities. It soon became clear how deeply sovereignty would be affected by state jurisdiction. The U.S. government wanted to get out of the Indian business, and its steps to realize this goal included relocating members, terminating their tribal governments, and extending state authority over Indians.

Red Lake developed and maintained its own criminal code, court system, and police force (through auspices of the Bureau of Indian Affairs). The federal government intervenes and assumes jurisdiction over major crimes, but the State of Minnesota has no authority at Red Lake. That is why, when a school shooting occurred there in 2005, for example, federal law enforcement agencies investigated. The Bois Forte Reservation (Minnesota) was initially subject to Public Law 280, but it succeeded in getting an exemption in 1975. It also maintains its own courts, police, and legal code. Bois Forte and Red Lake are now exploring ways to use their courts to exert jurisdiction over major crimes as well. In 2009, for example, a Bois Forte tribal member burned down the tribal headquarters and was charged with arson under the Major Crimes Act, but Bois Forte also charged him with arson in tribal court. The dual charge was not double jeopardy because the United States and Bois Forte are separate sovereigns under the law. This tactic has the potential to expand tribal jurisdiction and undermine the role of the Major Crimes Act in thwarting tribal sovereignty.

As tribes have become better educated about sovereignty and the law and better funded, most have begun to develop their own court systems and police forces. As of 2012, Fond du Lac is the only tribe in Minnesota that does not have its own court. A few have negotiated memoranda of agreement with state, county, and municipal law enforcement agencies. Pressure is mounting for a repeal of Public Law 280 or a case-by-case exemption for many reservations. Many tribes have also had success in legal challenges to the civil authority of states over Indians in Public Law 280, as demonstrated by *Bryan v. Itasca County* and other cases.[5]

Don't tribes ever investigate murders on Indian land themselves?

Yes. States have formal jurisdiction in murder cases where Public Law 280 is in effect, and the FBI has formal jurisdiction in murder cases in all other parts of Indian country. However, tribal police do a great deal of investigative and police work relative to murder and drug charges on reservations. Tribal police often exercise arrest and search warrants, cooperate with the FBI and other law enforcement agencies, and participate in joint task forces to make their communities safe.

Do Indians face racial profiling from law enforcement?

Racial profiling does still happen.[6] Whites can be sure that the color of their skin was not a factor in being pulled over for speed-

Red Lake (Minnesota) tribal justice complex

ing, but an Indian, especially one with tribal license plates, never knows for sure. Beltrami County (Minnesota) and Red Lake have had disagreements about exercising one another's arrest warrants, and the Beltrami County sheriff's office intentionally profiled Indians, pulling over cars with Red Lake plates to see if the subjects of the warrants were in the vehicles, using only the racial profile (tribal license plate) to decide whom to pull over and investigate. That problem is being actively addressed by the Beltrami County sheriff's office now.

In Minnesota, Indians comprise 1 percent of the state population and 17 percent of the state's prison population. But Indians are not seventeen times more likely to commit crimes. The system investigates, charges, tries, convicts, and incarcerates Indians at a rate much higher than the general population. There are some great people working in law enforcement today who are trying to change this situation, but clearly much more needs to be done. A 2010 Arizona law intended to combat illegal immigration allows police to pull over anyone who they have "reasonable suspicion" is an illegal immigrant, which many people believe has increased racial profiling of Indians and Mexicans.

Most Indians are policed by nonnative people. That's only a problem when race becomes a factor in how citizens are treated by law enforcement. Since race is a factor in many Indian cases, racial profiling continues to be a problem.

Should Leonard Peltier be freed?

In 1975, two FBI agents were murdered in South Dakota. This event occurred shortly after a major police and military action at Wounded Knee on the Pine Ridge Indian Reservation. Several different reports and investigations, well synthesized for the public in the video documentary *Incident at Oglala* and a special on *60 Minutes,* have now made it clear that the two most damaging pieces of evidence used to convict Leonard Peltier of the murders should not have been admissible in court. One was a ballistics report that was clearly fabricated by the FBI. The other was an affidavit from a woman named Myrtle Poor Bear, who later stated that the FBI coerced her by threatening to permanently remove her children from her home.

Many people feel that Leonard Peltier was made into a scapegoat and punished for a crime he did not commit. Those who argue for Leonard Peltier's release also often state that we owe it to the families of the FBI agents who were murdered to find

The American Indian Movement (Clyde Bellecourt, one of its leaders, shown here) gained international fame for its takeover of the Wounded Knee Trading Post and other acts of civil disobedience, but the things for which its members are less well known are most appreciated by the Indian community.

their true killers. If Leonard Peltier had received a fair trial or a retrial without the pieces of clearly tainted evidence, he probably would not have been convicted. But did he kill those FBI agents? Maybe not, but I don't know.

Is AIM good or bad?

I do not agree with everything that the American Indian Movement (AIM) or its leaders have done or said, but I do believe that AIM has done more good than bad. Ojibwe and other Indians in Minneapolis founded the American Indian Movement in 1968.[7] AIM was catapulted to national fame for its poignant protests. Some members participated in the takeover of the federal prison at Alcatraz in 1969, although they did not organize that event. AIM did organize a takeover of the Bureau of Indian Affairs in 1972. As a result, many Americans heard, felt, and understood Indian discontent with government policies for the first time, even though the protests did little to change policy.

AIM also got embroiled in reservation politics and the profoundly disturbing injustice of the American legal system through the Custer courthouse burning and the Wounded Knee Trading Post occupation in South Dakota in 1973. The organization's activism again raised the group's public profile and made known the issues that motivated it but did little to bring new government action or to address the underlying issues that caused so much unrest in the Indian community.

AIM's greatest achievements are the ones for which it is less well known nationally but far more appreciated by Indians.[8] AIM was initially created to deal with Indian urbanization and poverty in Minneapolis. In 1968 it founded the AIM Legal Rights Center, which provided free legal counsel and representation to Indians. More than thirty thousand people have been served by the legal center to date. In 1968 AIM also founded the AIM Patrol, which sought to police the police, document cases of police brutality and racial profiling, assist Indians with legal grievances, and advocate for victims of crimes. The AIM Patrol evolved over time: in 1986, when a serial killer was targeting Indian women in Minneapolis, the patrol provided free protective escorts for native women who needed to walk or ride to work, school, and shopping centers. In 1979 AIM also developed the American Indian Opportunities Industrialization Center, a very successful source of job training and placement for urban and reservation Indians.

The American Indian Movement also provided innovative leadership in education by pioneering the first Indian culture–based K–12 school in Minnesota. The Heart of the Earth Survival School was created in 1971, and it graduated more Indians than all of the other Minneapolis-area schools combined. Heart of the Earth underwent some serious struggles and eventually closed, but its historic achievements in serving urban Indian youth and inspiring other tribal school initiatives are remarkable.

What is the Indian Child Welfare Act?

The Indian Child Welfare Act (ICWA) sought to address a horrific problem in adoption and foster care of native children. Expert testimony presented at the legislative hearings for the act included surveys conducted by the Association on American Indian Affairs and other organizations indicating that as many as 35 percent of native children were separated from their homes by adoption or foster care.[9] In Minnesota, as much as 25 percent of the infant Indian population was being adopted. Minnesota's out-of-home placement rate for Indians was five times that of nonnative children. More than 90 percent of the adoption and foster placements were with non-Indian families. The trend disempowered parents in the raising of their own children and disconnected native youth from their families, reservations, and culture.

Social service agencies were plagued with oversight and procedural problems. Most of the native kids removed from their homes never had a social worker visit those homes. Racial bias was prevalent. Many tribal members were terrified of losing their children—not because they were bad parents but because they were Indian.

The 1978 Indian Child Welfare Act was the first serious legislative attempt to counteract these tendencies. It provided mandates to state courts and county social service case agencies for placement of children who were removed from their homes, prioritizing placement with (1) preference of the child and parent, (2) extended family, (3) other tribal members, and (4) other Indians. It also required that agencies notify tribes of cases affecting their members, and it granted tribal courts and agencies the right to intervene in their children's welfare.

ICWA was a big step in the right direction, but there were many problems with the law. First, it had no teeth: there were no fines, sanctions, or punishments for individuals or agencies that did not comply with the act. It was also difficult for caseworkers to know if a child was Indian and what tribe the child was enrolled in (or even if the child was enrolled) and to find qualified native homes for placement. Canadian Indians living in the United States and Indians whose tribal affiliation was not known were not covered by the act because they were not "federally recognized." The act also provided no means or guidance for education or training social service workers about native culture, history, language, or even the act itself.

All social service agencies were so grossly underfunded that even after passage of the act the trends were barely affected. Furthermore, while foster care placements usually involved a house visit by a social worker, even years after the act only a small percentage of the Indian foster care removals did. Legal processes also take time. Often tribes received no notice, or a late notice, and by the time they tried to intervene and advocate, the affected children had already been removed from their homes for two years or more.

Today, state social service agencies must develop permanency plans within one year of initiating litigation such as a CHIPS (Children in Need of Protective Services) petition, and communication between tribal and county agencies has greatly improved. Judges routinely query social service workers about site visits in many states as well. Some state and tribal governments signed memoranda of agreement that obligate states to pay for foster care placements ordered by tribal courts. Some states passed additional legislation, like the Minnesota Indian Family Preservation Act, which sought to strengthen and expand some provisions of ICWA. Minnesota saw a 92 percent decline in Indian adoptions and a 66 percent decline in the Indian foster care rate over the first two decades after ICWA. In spite of that dramatic improvement, the effects have been insufficient. Indians still have the highest foster care and adoption rates of all racial groups in the United States and in most states occupy a percentage of the caseload ten times their percentage of the overall population. Much more needs to be done to ensure tribal involvement in the process, racial sensitivity training and cultural education for county social service workers, reduction in unnecessary removals of Indian children, and connection of removed children to their communities and culture.

What is blood quantum, what is tribal enrollment, and how are they related?

Blood quantum is the percentage of a person's racial lineage that can be documented as Indian. Tribal governments keep lists of enrolled members, otherwise known as tribal citizens. Eligibility for enrollment in most tribes is dependent on blood quantum. This is the political definition of Indianness.

Blood quantum was first used in Virginia in the eighteenth century to restrict the rights of people with half or more native ancestry. By the 1930s, the federal government and many tribes were using blood quantum to determine who was eligible for tribal citizenship. The fractions are expressed up to sixty-fourths—one might have a quantum of 37/64.

Criteria for tribal citizenship vary from tribe to tribe. Some, like the Pueblo, are very exclusive. Others, like the St. Croix Ojibwe (Wisconsin), require prospective members to prove 50 percent Indian blood. Most tribes still require prospective members to prove that they have at least 25 percent Indian blood, although some will now accept lineal descent. Most tribes also do not acknowledge Indian blood from other tribes. Fathers who are not named on birth certificates or don't sign voluntary recognition of paternity papers do not have their blood counted.

There are many more self-identified Indians than enrolled members.[10] Some of those self-identified Indians have tenuous ties to native communities; they know only that someone way back in their family tree might have been Indian. Many other self-identified Indians grew up and now live in native communities, have dark skin, and even speak tribal languages—but are still not eligible for enrollment. The obstacle is that tribal citizenship is not determined by residence at time of birth, as for most nations, but rather by proof of a percentage of blood from a given tribe and a completed enrollment application.

Tribes have a clear right and responsibility to decide who belongs and who does not. The primary alternative to the racial basis of blood quantum as the determinant for membership is lineal descent: to open membership to those who can demonstrate that they have a direct Indian ancestor. But opening enrollment to more members might result in a flood of returnees, potentially allowing people who have never lived on the reservation to take over tribal politics and reduce the political power and economic resources of those who have lived there the longest. The tribes that have casinos and distribute per capita payments have further disincentive to expand tribal membership criteria, for fear of diluting benefits to current tribal members. In California, over 2,500 tribal members have been disenrolled by their tribes in recent years—and every one of those tribes operates a substantial casino.[11] The economic and political climate on reservations is inherently divisive just when it needs to be inclusive.

Unfortunately, the enrollment records used to determine blood quantum are highly flawed. The original blood quantum calculations at White Earth (Minnesota), for example, were compiled during a lawsuit over land fraud in the 1910s by eugenics-trained scientists Albert Jenks and Ales Hrdlicka, who measured head shape, analyzed hair thickness, and scratched enrollees' skin, noting pink marks as evidence of nonnative blood.[12] By reducing the number of official full bloods at White Earth from over 5,000 to 127, they vastly diminished the compensation that the U.S. government had to pay for land fraud. Amazingly, their lists—built on exactly those criteria—still comprise the database for determining blood quantum and tribal enrollment at White Earth today.[13]

There are people whose tribal enrollment records show a 100 percent blood quantum, meaning that, on paper, they are biologically 100 percent Indian. But many of those people have one relative way back in the family tree who is not Indian. There are many people whose tribal enrollment record says they are 25 percent Indian when they and their communities know for a fact that their blood quantum is much more. As a result of this arcane system, many Indians who by most measures would count as full-blooded cannot get enrolled.

While the Indian population in America is growing very rapidly, the enrolled population is advancing much more slowly and on the verge of declining on some reservations. A demographic report on the Salish and Kootenai tribes of the Flathead Reservation (Montana) showed that the death rate has now eclipsed the enrollment rate and a current slow decline in the enrolled population will accelerate significantly after 2020.[14] The tribes appear to be breeding themselves into extinction, completing what forced assimilation could not accomplish. It is a tremendous source of frustration for many Indians who want to belong to, vote for, and serve their tribes and people as bona fide members, but cannot. The net result is that more than half of America's self-identified Indian people suffer the drawbacks of societal discrimination and their pernicious history and current community dysfunction but enjoy none of the benefits of tribal membership. And the debate about identity fuels the bad feelings and paralysis that have plagued tribes for decades.

Blood is part of identity, but the stuff on the inside matters more than exterior color, hair type, and height of cheekbone. Participation in culture and knowledge of the tribal language do not directly correlate to one's percentage of Indian blood, and these things often impact identity, tell us who we are, more deeply than color. By extending the privileges of tribal citizenship only to those who have a certain racial pedigree and ignoring all other variables of identity, tribes are actually participating in racism. They are alienating and excluding not just non-Indians but also identifiable Indians who have Indian blood, language, and culture. That is not okay.

Many Indians believe that if tribes are ever going to be effective in attacking the root of the problems that plague their communities, they must open the doors to tribal membership for all their people.[15] Concerns about being overrun by newcomers could be somewhat mitigated by making prospective members apply in person on the reservation. In New Zealand, Australia, South America, and Central America, blood quantum has never been the primary measure of legitimacy or citizenship for tribal peoples, and its absence has not harmed indigenous people. In the United States, the most important questions for an Indian tribe are not about us as a race. They are about us as nations.

How has tribal enrollment affected you personally?

I am not an enrolled member of any tribe, although I have enrolled relatives from Leech Lake, White Earth, Mille Lacs, and Red Lake reservations in Minnesota. But errors in enrollment records can be corrected, and I have hopes of being enrolled eventually, either at Leech Lake (where my ancestral village of Bena is located and most of my family is from) or White Earth (where my mother is enrolled).

For you to understand the depths of this question in the lives of Indians who are not enrolled, though, it's easiest for me to simply tell you about my children. We have a large blended family, with nine children who don't all have the same biological parents. They are all identifiably native in appearance, and they have grown up around Ojibwe ceremonies, language, and lifeways—snaring rabbits, harvesting wild rice, and processing maple syrup. For all of them, being Indian is something you are, believe, and do. It has nothing to do with a piece of paper or blood quantum. They don't even know what blood quantum is. But three of my children are enrolled members at Leech Lake and six are ineligible for enrollment.

They learned about enrollment very young, though. One year I took the kids to Leech Lake's community Christmas party. When they lined up with other reservation children to receive a gift "from Santa," tribal employees handed one present to each of my children on the tribal enrollment list and told their un-enrolled siblings that they could not receive a gift. Being rejected by anyone is painful, but being rejected by the people with whom you identify most strongly and the community or government that represents them is excruciating. For the rest of their lives, three of my children will get to vote in tribal elec-tions, receive modest college scholarship assistance from the tribe, and participate in the tribal fish harvest. Six will not. Three will be eligible to run for tribal office. Six will not. My beautiful, smart kids are some of the most culturally knowl-edgeable people of their generation, so Leech Lake loses too, because only three of these incredible kids get to represent the tribe as bona fide members.

Enrolled or not, all of my children know who they are, but I cannot protect them all from the very tangible pain of exclu-sion by their own tribe—exclusion from a petty Christmas ritu-al, yes, and from the deep sense of belonging that accompanies tribal citizenship.

How come some tribes ban the use and sale of alcohol?

The U.S. federal government used to regulate—and for a long time prohibit—the sale of alcohol on Indian land. Some of the tribal prohibitions against alcohol stem from old U.S. Indian liquor laws. However, in this day and age, it is up to each tribal government to decide whether to ban the sale of alcohol on their land. Many tribes have removed the restriction. Some have removed it recently, with the advent of tribal gaming operations, hoping to lure more patrons to "wet" casinos. In other places, tribal leadership and their constituencies have insisted that their reservations remain "dry." In addition to the problems that many native communities have with substance abuse, many tribal members see alcohol consumption as a practice contrary to traditional cultural values.

Is there a solution to substance abuse in Indian country?

There is no easy answer. If there were, we wouldn't have a problem. Contemporary issues of poverty, joblessness, historical trauma, violence, and substance abuse are all deeply intertwined. It is impossible to target one of those issues effectively without addressing all of the others. Indians and non-Indians alike have been scratching their heads for decades without making major progress on curbing substance abuse.

The most promising solutions we have lie in the realm of cultural revitalization. Decades upon decades of consistent effort to assimilate Indians have damaged native communities in horrifying ways. The more disconnected native people have become from their motherlands, languages, and cultural ways, the more dysfunctional they have become. And as outsiders have attempted to change Indians over the years, Indians have felt more and more isolated and misunderstood. This helps explain why culturally based treatment programs are significantly more successful for Indian addicts than mainstream ones.[16] In a few places, concerted broad-based efforts have revitalized traditional tribal language and culture. In those places, we often see a parallel strengthening of community cohesion, declining rates of substance abuse, and improvement in academic achievement.

For native communities, these examples are the most promising effort to bring meaningful solutions to the people. For others, it is important to realize that America's greatest strength and greatest potential in helping Indians lies not in attempting to assimilate and integrate them further but rather in respecting and supporting the cultural and linguistic diversity that makes this country truly great.

Do all Indians have drinking problems?

No, but a lot of people have a problem seeing it that way. If someone walks into a crowded bar and sees two hundred inebriated white college students, they do not say, "See, all white people are drunks." But if someone walks into the same bar and sees two hundred inebriated white college students and one inebriated Indian, it is reasonably likely that he or she would at least think if not say the same about Native Americans.

Over the Thanksgiving holiday in 2010, Station 280 (a St. Paul, Minnesota, bar) produced a poster featuring a scantily clad Native American woman posing provocatively in front of a drawing of a happy cowboy with his arm around an Indian man who was passed out drunk. The poster read, "Drink Like an Indian, Party Like a Pilgrim." The poster encapsulated negative stereotypes about Indians and alcohol—that Indians have drinking problems, that Indian men can't handle their liquor but white men can—with the additional gratuitous sexual objectification of Indian women.

The stereotypes about alcoholism and Indians are complicated by the reality. Substance abuse is a problem in Indian country. We cannot rewrite history, nor can we rewrite well-documented statistics. Many reasons explain the issue of widespread substance abuse in the tribal population. The evidence about genetic predisposition to alcoholism is conflicting and not always conclusive. However, environmental elements, historical factors, and issues of poverty all play heavily into this problem.

At the same time that there is a problem with substance abuse in Indian country, it surprises some people to know that a large percentage of the U.S. tribal population abstains entirely from the use of alcohol. For many tribes, alcohol is considered taboo in traditional ceremonial circles. That, along with the fact that there are many recovering alcoholics in Indian country, has led a large percentage of the population to abstain from alcohol use of any kind. It also means that when Indian people are true to their beliefs and customs, they can find value systems and places that support and reinforce the culture of mental and physical health, free from substance abuse.

The pervasive negative stereotype of the drunken Indian strengthens an indigenous sense of otherness and dislocation from mainstream society. And because traditional ceremonial lifestyles and belief systems are threatened in many places, many native youth have internalized negative stereotypes of themselves. It is not sufficient to tell native kids to be proud of who they are if we do not also at the same time tell them who they are. The struggle in connecting young people to their traditions is compounded by a school system that consistently provides opportunities to learn about others but very few for native kids to learn about themselves. We have a lot of work to do.

Why is there so much concern about mascots?

Not all Indians find the use of Indians or Indian imagery by sports teams offensive, but many do. They view nonnative people dressed as Indians, doing a "tomahawk chop," or singing fake Indian songs as a mockery of their culture and history. Those opposed to the use of Indians as mascots usually point out that most people would not tolerate white sports fans dressed up in fake Afros singing mock African songs for a sports team using a stereotype of black people as a mascot. The protest against using nonnative racial groups as mascots has been so overwhelming that the practice was universally abandoned. In Red Wing (Minnesota), in 2008 and 2009, sixty to seventy white students dressed in low-slung pants and sports jerseys and flashed gang signs in a caricature of black culture the students called "Wigger Day."[17] A lawsuit was filed that resulted in school officials actively discouraging and suppressing the custom, with some resistance from students. But similar caricatures of Indians in other places have often been widely defended by school officials and community members, even officially celebrated as part of the sports culture at the schools.

The two biggest defenses of Indian mascots are pretty weak. The first is the claim that "we are honoring Native Americans." If all Native Americans felt honored, then that argument would bear some weight, but most do not feel honored. And even if a home team truly believes it is honoring Indians through its mascot, opposing teams caricature and abuse each other's mas-

In 1992, a large crowd gathered to protest the use of Native Americans as mascots during the Super Bowl between the Buffalo Bills and the Washington Redskins. So far, the NFL and its teams have been unwilling to address the issue.

cots in the name of team spirit. Thus, other teams in the same conference with a team that has a native mascot will most definitely *not* be honoring them.

Nonnative people also justify the practice by pointing to Indians who use Indian mascots for teams, such as the Red Lake Warriors. The difference is that the Indians at Red Lake are the descendants of warriors, so their use of that image or name is not a mockery. However, I never miss a chance to encourage Red Lake and other native schools to change their mascots to something more benign so that it does not confuse others about appropriate mascots. The bottom line is that if any mascot is truly offensive to a large percentage of the population, then that mascot should go. Stick to lions, tigers, and bears. Human beings will never feel dishonored by that.

Why don't tribes do more to support language and culture?

This is a very important question, and because it touches my work, I have some strong opinions on the topic. Language and culture receive little more than token support in many places, even where language and culture are strong enough to warrant an intervention that has a good chance of preserving and revitalizing tribal societies.

Priorities compete for tribal support. Poverty is a real problem in most Indian communities in the United States and Canada, and many tribes have well-designed and much-needed programs to combat it. But tribal governments also spend a lot of money on powwows and charitable donations to nonnative organizations like churches—a painful irony. For most tribes, powwows are a new cultural form, one that did not come from their people. And churches and missionary organizations were at the forefront of efforts to assimilate and change Native Americans. Their role in advocating for removal to reservations and their participation in the residential boarding school experiment did tremendous damage to many Indian people and communities. But it's relatively easy to support a local powwow that people understand and enjoy and to give money to a church that many tribal leaders and members belong to.

Learning a tribal language is hard. Many tribes have very few or no speakers left, making prioritizing tribal language or ancient cultural ways much more difficult. Indian cultures and identities are changing very rapidly. Many tribal members find it easier to redefine what it means to be Indian, with greater emphasis on things like holding a tribal enrollment card, rather than trying to preserve and revitalize cultural forms and a concept of identity that is more recognizable to their ancestors.

Supporting tribal language and culture also involves taking a good hard look at one's self and community. Exploring this dynamic is especially important because it is language and culture revitalization that offer our greatest opportunities for strengthening political, economic, educational, and community health.

Why are Indian politics often such a viper's pit?

Why are American politics such a viper's pit? Political processes and politicians everywhere evolve in a contentious world, but there are additional complications in Indian country. Indian communities are small, and tribal leaders, while responsible to all tribal members, trust and rely upon their extended families with big responsibilities. That dynamic is not a bad thing by itself, but in many places its effect is a high turnover rate in tribal government jobs and an electoral process that is not just loaded with the angst and hope of voters who care about the political and economic future of their people but of tribal citizens who are worried about their personal job security.

The biggest problem in tribal politics has very little to do with people and much more to do with the structure of tribal government today. The U.S. constitution provides checks and balances. If the president does something outrageous or illegal, he can be impeached. The courts can check legislation and make sure that laws are not onerous or oppressive. The executive and legislative branches have to work together and come to agreement on spending money. But most tribes were given constitutions by the U.S. government that were drafted on a corporate governance model, without effective checks and balances. In many of those places, if the tribal chair is accused of malfeasance and the court rules against the tribal chair, the tribal chair can then appoint an appellate judge, with no need for approval, and see to it that the appellate judge overrules the lower court's decision.

Many tribes have effectively revised the constitutions that the U.S. government handed to them. But constitutional reform is difficult and contentious for any government. And many tribal governments have yet to effectively reform their structure to provide for greater checks and balances. Without an effective system of checks and balances inherent in the structure of the tribal governments, things function well when tribal leadership has impeccable integrity, but things fall apart when someone does not. Tribal leaders are no more prone to corruption than any politician in the American system—but they are also no less prone. The primary difference is in the structure of the governments.

The other problem with politics in Indian country is that indigenous values and leadership structures are not at the center of tribal politics. In many places, hereditary chiefs from numerous communities were smashed together in one small place. Nobody would be chief of them all. And the fault lines, factions, and cliques that plague many Indian communities today had their beginnings at the start of the reservation period, with the very identities of the people. Combine that with the fact that the modern world involves networking with the U.S. government, the Bureau of Indian Affairs, and many other political and financial institutions.

Tribal politics are complicated. The work involves an understanding of financial and legal contracts. Yet the constituents to which tribal leaders are responsible are often unfamiliar with and especially untrusting of those institutions and processes. This distrust makes it far easier for tribal leaders to be misunderstood or demonized. And it also makes it easier for tribal leaders, some of whom are unfamiliar with modern financial and political processes themselves, to make mistakes.

In spite of all those pressures and complications, there are still many wonderful tribal leaders who have worked through the problems with great integrity and helped make their communities safer, healthier, and more prosperous. That's pretty amazing.

Are tribes getting better?

Yes, things are getting better. The political and economic power of native nations has grown tremendously, especially following the advent of casino gaming. Tribal leaders are more astute and effective operating in the American political system, and the American public has become slightly more aware of and knowledgeable about what is happening in Indian country, which helps generate outside support.

In spite of all that, there remains an incredible amount of work to be done. While poverty and substance abuse still plague most Indian communities, they may not be the greatest threats to survival. The Seminole (Florida), for example, have eliminated poverty for their people. They were even able to write a check to the state of Florida to help fill a major shortfall in the education budget for the entire state, which of course bought them a great deal of love from their nonnative neighbors. But if you ask the Seminole what keeps them up at night, they usually respond, "Language and culture loss."

Tribal leaders across the land work very hard, many of them with great integrity, to climb the mountain to political empowerment and financial prosperity. While these are worthy goals, my fear is that they will manage to climb that mountain to the very top, look around, and say, "Oh my god, we just climbed the wrong mountain. We should have been climbing the mountain of language and culture revitalization while we had the chance, while we had the speakers and the cultural carriers and the opportunity." After all, why would we need sovereignty and tribal government if we were completely assimilated with the rest of America? And if Indians have a hard time answering that question satisfactorily to other Indians, they're going to have a really hard time answering it to the rest of America.

Why do Indians have so many kids?

Throughout history, many ethnic or racial enclaves have been famous for their large families. For Indians, it is true that many tribes have a culturally ingrained love of family. But the same can also be said for many cultures across the globe. The larger family size in many parts of Indian country is less because of culture and more because of other variables. All disproportionately poor subsections of the population tend to have children at a younger age and more often.

Access to and knowledge of birth control, combined with pre- and postnatal care, have improved dramatically over the past several decades in Indian country. The birth rate is moderating. The trends that have slowed the birth rate throughout the industrialized world are slowly changing and reducing the birthrate in Indian country too. Having six children or more in a family was very common for the grandparent generation and even many people in the parental generation but is quite rare for Indians who are raising young families today.

I heard that a lot of Indians serve in the U.S. military. How do they reconcile their service with the fact that the U.S. Army killed so many of their people?

Indian people have fought in every American war from the Revolution to Afghanistan. And Indians have served in the U.S. armed forces in larger numbers on a per capita basis than any other racial group in every conflict since World War I, before they were even U.S. citizens. Many Native Americans enlisted for financial reasons. Poverty has been and remains prevalent in most Indian communities. The service was a way to earn money, provide for one's family, and escape from despair on the reservations. Many servicemen also seek a place in their families' military histories and the bonds of brotherhood that can only be forged in combat. Many tribes have long, storied military traditions, and serving in the armed forces is also a way to gain respect within their tribes and use the vaunted position of warrior to speak at ceremonies, carry eagle staffs and flags at powwows, and remind others of their people's proud warrior heritage.

Native soldiers are typically well aware that the flag they serve under also persecuted Indians and many others throughout its history, but they serve the U.S. military proudly. According to Gulf War veteran and Mille Lacs (Minnesota) tribal member Sean Fahrlander, "I said that if I have to protect white people in order to protect my people, I'll do it. Don't ever forget—this *land* is still my country."[18]

How do Indians feel about the use of *Geronimo* as the code name for Osama Bin Laden?

On May 2, 2011, U.S. Navy SEALs killed Osama Bin Laden, architect of the 9/11 terror strikes against America. The U.S. military used *Geronimo* as the code name for Bin Laden in that action. Audio snippets from the raid included the lines, "We have a visual on Geronimo," and "Geronimo is K.I.A."

The real Geronimo was a legendary leader among the Apache and remains an iconic symbol of Indian resistance, pride, and power to many native people. Many Indians viewed the code name as a slap in the face and an effort to recast a tribal hero into the role of villain, terrorist, and enemy of the United States. The use of *Geronimo* as Bin Laden's code name may have been a thoughtless blunder on the military's part, but that oversight hurt the morale of many native soldiers, who still serve in the U.S. military in higher numbers on a per capita basis than any other racial group in the country.

When I heard the use of the code name in the media coverage right after Bin Laden's death, I immediately thought of my grandfather, Eugene Seelye, who enlisted in the U.S. Army, putting his life on the line and earning a Purple Heart storming Omaha Beach during World War II. He gave so much to his country, and I wondered when his country would drop its callous disregard for Indians and reciprocate with a little respect.

Economics

"Money is like health. Having it is no
guarantee of happiness. But the absence
of it can make one miserable."

SUZE ORMAN

Do Indians get a break on taxes, and if so, why?

Some Indians do get a break on some taxes—but of course, it's
complicated. All Indians, whether they are enrolled members
or not, must pay federal income tax. All Indians must also pay
property taxes in the county or municipality in which they own
a house—unless they live on tribal trust land, which is the case
for a small percentage of Indian people. All Indians must also
pay state income tax unless they are enrolled members who obtain all of their income from their tribe and live on their reservation, leaving only a small number of Indians exempt from
state income tax. In Minnesota, for example, only 23 percent of
enrolled Indians live on a reservation.[1] Only some of those obtain all their income from that reservation. All Indians also pay
sales tax on everything other Americans do with the exception
of vehicles (see page 129).

The reasons for these complex tax rules lie in history. Essentially, a state government has no jurisdiction over Indians
on Indian land unless the federal government specifically
gives that authority to states. That is why Indians living on
Indian land pay federal but not state income tax. Many tribes

have negotiated compacts with the states in which they are located by which those tribes agree to pay other state taxes such as sales tax in return for a monetary payment from the state government.

Many Americans feel that it is simply unfair that Indians should not be taxed on all things in all the ways that most Americans are taxed. And unfairness seems very un-American to them. Most Indians counter that there is nothing in their entire history that was fair to them. When weighed against traumas from the loss of the land to assimilation policies to the way that the government continues to ignore poverty in Indian country, the small tax benefits that go to a small percentage of tribal members hardly seems worth fussing about. Tribal leaders also frequently point out that they supply many in-kind services to nonnative people by plowing roads, providing police protection and fire service on reservation lands where many nonnative people live, and bearing the expense for those services to tribal members that county and state governments would be obligated to provide if the tribes did not.

Both opponents and supporters are unaware that any significant change to the tax status of Indians would require revisiting the U.S. constitution and many of the treaties the United States signed with Indian nations. Opening those legal processes would probably cost the U.S. government and its taxpaying citizens far more money than they would save by living with the status quo. The special tax status of tribal members is part of the structure and payment that the United States had to agree to in order to obtain the rest of America from Indians. There is no way to redo one without redoing the other.

Do Indians get a break on license plates?

Indian nations are exempt from the authority of state governments with the exception of jurisdiction shifts in places where Public Law 280 is in effect (see page 104). For this reason, many tribes license motor vehicles independently from state agencies. State governments, wanting to get their hands on some of the revenue stream and keep records of all tribal vehicles in the state system for purposes of law enforcement, have negotiated compacts with tribal governments in many places by which state governments enable and support tribal vehicle licensing (with some limitations). As a result, enrolled tribal citizens can exempt themselves from state vehicle sales tax if the automobile dealer agrees to deliver the vehicle to the tribal member on the reservation. They can also obtain and renew license plates at a subsidized rate.

Tribal license plates are an affirmation of sovereignty for many Indians but sometimes a bone of contention as well. Many tribal members feel they are targeted for racial profiling by their distinctive license plates.

Why should Indians be eligible for welfare if they are not taxed the same way as everyone else?

Indians are U.S. citizens and shouldn't be denied the benefits of other citizens because of their race. Further, the U.S. federal government has legal obligations to provide for the health, education, and welfare of American Indians. Reneging on that responsibility would be not only morally but legally problematic. And finally, funds and benefits to citizens of any given state are distributed through auspices of county social service agencies but are not paid for by county or state government. Welfare benefits are paid for by the U.S. federal government and sent to states in block grants to distribute to their citizens. Because Indians are not exempt from federal taxation, it is bogus to assert that they are not paying into the pool that finances welfare.

In addition, a great nation can only be as happy as its least happy citizens. When the unemployment rate in the United States reached a sustained level over 15 percent in the 1930s, they called it the Great Depression. Massive public policy initiatives sought to remedy the nation's economic woes. Well, the unemployment rate in Indian country has never been below 15 percent. For Indians, the "Great Depression" began in the nineteenth century, and it has never ended. The unemployment rate in many communities averages 50 percent, although most see rates around 20 percent. While a couple of tribes have successfully eliminated poverty, they are the exception, not the rule. And the fact that the first Americans continue to suffer so much makes a sad and untenable statement about the health of American democracy. We should be doing more for Indians, not less.

Are all Indians living in extreme poverty?

No. Some tribes, such as the Pequot (Connecticut), the Seminole (Florida), and the Mdewakanton Dakota (Minnesota), have successfully eliminated poverty for all of their enrolled tribal citizens. Many other tribes have successfully reduced the unemployment rate from 50 to 20 percent. This dramatic improvement has largely been brought about by casino gaming. But any place where 20 percent of the population is unemployed has a problem. In Nevada and South Dakota, tribal gaming enterprises are not monopolies, and unemployment is 50 percent or higher in many tribal communities. So, there is a diversity of experience with poverty for Indian people in the United States today. A few groups are well-off. Many groups are improving but are still disproportionately poor. And some groups still have most of their citizens living in abject poverty.

Are all Indians rich from casinos?

As stated above, a few groups are well-off, many groups are improving but still disproportionately poor, and some groups have most of their citizens living in abject poverty. The advent of casino gaming has affected some Native Americans far more than others. For tribes that have a monopoly on gaming in a given region and a very small number of tribal members, casinos have provided a dramatic impact on their members' financial status. But for most Indians who live in rural areas or come from tribes with large numbers of members, the impact has been much smaller.

Each tribe is an independent nation, with no legal obligations to other tribes. Casino profits are not shared by all tribes in America. Wealthy tribes often engage in philanthropy with less fortunate tribes, and in Wisconsin all tribes agreed to share a small percentage of revenues. But those developments have not come close to leveling the dramatic wealth disparities among tribes, even in Wisconsin.

How has casino gambling affected Indian communities?

Gaming and gambling are not governed by federal statutes, which is why some states like Nevada and South Dakota have legalized many forms of gambling but others, like Minnesota, have not. Indian gaming got its start in the late 1970s when the Seminole Indians of Florida ignored the state's gaming laws (which allowed church bingo but nothing more) and developed a high-stakes bingo operation. The local sheriff tried to shut it down, but the tribe filed for an injunction, which was appealed all the way to the Fifth Circuit Court of Appeals. The decision, *Seminole Tribe of Florida v. Robert Butterworth* (1981), upheld the right of the Seminole to develop gaming operations without regard to state laws. It was another sovereignty victory for tribal governments and a huge eye-opener for tribes in states that had not legalized casino gambling.[2]

Legal challenges to tribal gaming persisted after *Seminole v. Butterworth*. However, the U.S. Supreme Court ruled in *California v. Cabazon Band of Mission Indians* (1987) that California could not regulate gaming on Indian land when it allowed gaming elsewhere in the state. *Cabazon* removed the final obstacles, and tribal gaming proliferated across the country. Within two years, hundreds of Indian nations developed some type of high-stakes bingo or casino-style gaming operation.

Many Indians worry about negative impacts of gaming on tribal members because they disproportionately patronize the casinos. Increased rates of gambling addiction, exposure to secondhand cigarette smoke, and what many view as an unhealthy and untraditional environment in the casinos are among the greatest worries. There is also significant concern about the misinformed assumption that "all Indians are rich from casinos" (see page 132), which has led many granting agencies and regular citizens to believe that tribes do not need outside help in fighting poverty or developing programs. The influx of money to tribes through gaming has also increased internal political strife and accusations of mismanagement and embezzlement. Some of those accusations are well founded; others are not.

The Mille Lacs Ojibwe (Minnesota) used casino income to build a new health clinic and new schools, establish an all-band-member retirement plan, purchase health insurance for all tribal members, purchase a bank and small businesses—and still save half of their casino revenues. The financial and political power they wield speaks well for the potential development of gaming operations in Indian country. It is up to tribal members and their governments to make the decisions they believe are best for them.

How have per capita payments affected Indian communities?

Per capita payments comprise a percentage of casino profits or a fixed amount of money distributed to every member of a tribe. Most tribes will probably never be able to offer them, since they have so many tribal members relative to their income stream from gaming. However, some communities with small populations and large casino operations have recently begun to pay a portion of their casino proceeds directly to tribal members.

The payments create huge dilemmas for tribal governments and members. Members want the payments, and they pressure or vote in leaders who promise to start and increase them. The policy often puts undue stress on the bottom line for tribes that stretch margins to make per capita payments and diverts revenue from deserving programs (health, education, housing). It becomes a catch-22 situation for tribal officials who find it politically impossible to reduce per capita payments but difficult to expand other businesses and programs when significant funds are diverted to the per capita payments.

For recipients, the payments are well-intended and welcome assistance, but some feel that per capita payments are a double-edged sword that does more harm than good. Tribes often put aside per capita payments for minors and give them large lump-sum payments at age eighteen. This timing accelerates negative behavior for some youth, who want to party with the largest check they have ever received, and often provides a disincentive for further education or career development. In addition, tribal members who used to augment their income and feed their families by harvesting wild rice, berries, and fish and by gardening, but now receive per capita payments, are far less likely to participate in those traditional lifeways, providing another disincentive to healthy living and further eroding traditional culture. Moreover, other tribes that can't really afford to make per capita payments have actually been exploring ways to cut spending on social services and education in order to make per capita payments in response to tribal member demand.

What is the future of Indian gaming?

I believe Indian gaming will not last forever. It will not end because politicians hate Indians but because they see opportunity. The economic and political climate in the United States has made it very difficult for both Democrats and Republicans to accomplish their campaign objectives without committing political suicide. Democrats can only raise taxes so high before they get voted out of office; Republicans can only cut education and entitlements so much before they get voted out of office. It is far easier for both parties to compete with Indian gaming at the state level. I believe state governments will increasingly develop and expand gaming enterprises to bridge revenue shortfalls, which will cause Indian gaming to be less profitable due to increased competition. The political backlash in Indian country is far easier for most politicians to deal with than the potential backlash from the general public for doing other things.

What should tribes be doing to improve the economic condition of their citizens?

Tribal governments are working hard to advance the economic well-being of their communities. Gaming has obviously given them a major boost over the past twenty years. My primary frustration with the business development plans of many tribal governments is that they often do not think beyond the casino doors. There are exceptions, of course, such as the Sault

Ste. Marie Ojibwe (Michigan), who operate over thirty different businesses. I believe state governments will be directly competing with tribes in the gaming industry and that the revenue stream will slowly decline. Tribes should look elsewhere for opportunities.

Tribes have a very special tax status in the United States. Pharmaceutical corporations go to Puerto Rico, where they have a preferable tax status. I would like to see tribal governments trying to bring that kind of business to reservations. It would generate numerous jobs, and most of those jobs would pay well. It would also enable tribes to diversify their business investments.

Many tribes are trying to expand their business models outside the gaming industry in ways that support cultural practices. Red Lake Fisheries (Minnesota) manages and processes fish harvested in tribal waters.

There's much more to improving the economic well-being of an entire people than a sound business plan. America remains the richest nation on earth, but its citizens have not all been rewarded equally. Wealthy tribal nations have not always succeeded in raising the standard of living for all of their citizens, either. In addition to a sound business plan with a diversified array of enterprises, tribal governments should provide strategic assistance with education, health care, and housing to augment state and federal programs. They need not provide direct handouts but should give support that incentivizes healthy living and self-sufficiency.

There is an entitlement mentality in Indian country that I see as a problem. At Leech Lake (Minnesota), for example, the tribe pays for all band member funerals. While the assistance is welcome and expected by all tribal members, that benefit uses up so much tribal revenue that it hinders the ability of the tribe to provide other services. It would be political suicide for anyone in the tribal government to stop that program. But support for health, education, language, and culture programs is even more important. Many entitlements are extended for all tribal members, not just those in financial need. What seems fair actually deprives some tribes of resources to help those who need it most. Many other tribes make similar decisions with their money. And while the federal government treated Indians unfairly in many different ways, we cannot afford to sit around and complain about it. We need to do something about it.

Education

"There are but two lasting bequests we
can hope to give our children. One of
these is roots, the other, wings."

HODDING CARTER

What were federal residential boarding schools?

One of the most pernicious dimensions of the war on Indian
culture was the residential boarding school system.[1] Beginning
in the late nineteenth century, missionary, military, and government officials advocated for the removal of Indian children
from their homes to better instruct them in the English language and American culture. Captain Richard Henry Pratt, su-
perintendent of the Carlisle Indian Industrial School in Pennsylvania, the first of many Indian boarding schools, said, "Our
goal is to kill the Indian in order to save the man."[2] The idea of
the schools had less to do with giving children an education
than it did with taking away their culture. Children were sent
to schools as far from home as possible in order to discour-
age runaways and inhibit parental contact. Their clothes were
burned and their hair cut. They were strictly forbidden to speak
tribal languages. At Carlisle and many other schools, children
spent half the day working in fields or digging ditches and half
the day in class. Attendance at Bureau of Indian Affairs (BIA)
boarding schools or church mission schools was compulsory for
Indian children—homeschooling and public schools were not
options for most Indian youth in the late nineteenth century.

The schools came under criticism after many children began to die from malnutrition and diseases like tuberculosis; their bodies were not sent home for burial. The commissioner of Indian Affairs defended the situation in 1899, saying, "This education policy is based on the well known inferiority of the great mass of Indians in religion, intelligence, morals, and home life."[3] There were twenty-five such schools in operation that year, with over twenty thousand students every year. Parents did have the option of sending their children to mission schools instead, but those schools were usually just as harsh in suppressing tribal languages and culture and even more likely to expose students to sexual molestation, which was commonly reported.[4] Problems were not immediately apparent to parents, who often initially thought that their children would receive opportunities upon graduation and at least three meals a day at the schools, which was more than many families could provide.

The experience was devastating for most families. On returning home, many children could no longer recognize their

Ojibwe and other Indian students at Carlisle Indian Industrial School, Pennsylvania

own parents and could not speak the same language. The economic opportunities advocates hoped would be available for
graduates never materialized in the country's racially polarized
climate. Children often felt they could not fit in either on or
off the reservations, and those feelings, together with the dire
poverty prevailing in most places, simply added to the growing
social dysfunction on the reservations.

The schools came under increasing scrutiny and attack as
more than half the children at Carlisle had trachoma by 1900
and an influenza outbreak at Haskell (Kansas) in 1918 killed
more than three hundred students.[5] Official modifications did
not change the dynamic, and Carlisle closed in 1918, but other
schools actually continued to increase their enrollments. In
1928, the U.S. government commissioned the Merriam Report,
which blasted the schools for poor nutrition and health care
for students, insufficient clothing, exceedingly harsh physical
punishment, and the breakup of tribal families. The next commissioner of Indian Affairs, John Collier, began to dismantle
and reform the BIA school system. It took many years, but after
World War II, day schools started to dominate the educational
experience of Indian children in the United States. Four BIA-
operated boarding schools are still in existence today, but their
policies have been thoroughly reformed.

The long-term effects of the residential boarding school
system are profound. People learn how to parent by how they
are parented, but with as many as three generations of Indians
going through BIA boarding schools, a critical piece of the social fabric was severely damaged. Many native families have re-
bounded from the effects of boarding schools, but their blessings
are derived in spite of the system rather than because of it. Of
the remaining 180 tribal languages spoken in the United States,
160 are likely to go extinct in the next thirty years because only
elders speak those languages.[6] Residential boarding schools are
one of the primary causal factors in this development.

One of the preeminent goals of the residential boarding
school system—educational achievement for native youth—

was directly countermanded by the policy itself. Many Indian people developed or deepened distrust of people in positions of governmental or educational power as a result of their experiences in residential boarding schools. Today there is an astounding achievement gap for Native American youth. One of the reasons is the distrust many family members have of the institutions that seek to educate. Many native parents do not feel comfortable at school conferences and choose not to attend, limiting their ability to provide positive intervention or support for teachers in bettering their children's education. If the residential boarding school experience had not crushed and alienated so many Native Americans, this dimension of the modern educational experience for Indians would be very different.

How come 50 percent of Indians are flunking their state-mandated tests in English and math?

There is an achievement gap for many subsections of the population in America, but, on closer examination, the "achievement gap" is really an "opportunity gap." Poverty is one of the factors that strongly contributes to that gap. Children growing up in poverty are far more likely to have a whole set of social variables that hinder their advancement in educational institutions. Most of these causes and effects are very well documented. For black American youth, education for a very long time was an opportunity unfairly denied. Native American youth carry the pernicious history of residential boarding schools and historical trauma: education was a tool used to assimilate. As a result, many Indians rightly question whether modern education is still designed to assimilate. When I went to school, I often heard from my native peers that my education, especially toward my advanced degrees, was an indicator of assimilation. I was called an "apple"—red on the outside but white inside—because I was well educated.

In addition, the modern educational system has been more sensitive and responsive to the black and Hispanic communities in revising curricula, perhaps because their numbers are so much greater. That is not to say that curricula is perfectly responsive to blacks or Hispanics. But there are strands in the social studies curricula for most states that require education about topics like the civil rights movement. Yet all that one can be sure of learning about Indians is a sugarcoated version of Christopher Columbus and Thanksgiving (see page 29). As a result, the curricula employed in most American schools is still largely about assimilation when it comes to Indians.

It is not the intent of those who develop state curriculum guidelines to alienate anyone or limit their opportunities, but that is exactly what happens in Indian country. An Indian student in the modern educational system will navigate many curricular strands before high school, but the teaching about the people who made America great (not them), the heroes, presidents, and cultural icons (not theirs), the success stories (not theirs), the culture and history of great civilizations (not theirs) serves to engineer a blow to self-esteem. The omission of Indians from the curriculum means that Indian children can go to school and learn all about the rest of the world but nothing about themselves.

The opportunity to learn about one's self is not the only gap that negatively affects the performance of native kids in school. The skill sets emphasized in modern education (math and reading) are great for some things and from some perspectives— but not all. Native people often have different values, different skill sets of emphasis, different learning styles, and different cultures. None of those differences are well supported in the modern educational system. All of these factors contribute to the opportunity gap for native youth.

Is there anything that works in the effort to bridge the achievement gap?

Some schools run by tribes and the Bureau of Indian Education meet No Child Left Behind requirements every year. But throughout the United States, Indian youth underperform and underachieve in many places. Often, only half the Indian youth in a given school district are passing their state-mandated tests in English and in math. Everyone is scratching their heads trying to figure out how to remedy the situation.

To me, the answer is quite simple. We need to transform the schools that educate Indian youth from schools designed to assimilate (and to teach curricula designed to assimilate) into schools that enable people to learn about themselves and the rest of the world. This approach is a big part of the success for tribal schools that are making the grade on state-mandated tests. In Wisconsin, an Ojibwe language immersion school called Waadookodaading has had a 100 percent pass rate on state-mandated tests in English administered in English for ten years in a row. But the teachers there never instruct native youth in anything other than the tribal language until the highest grades. That says a lot. And we should all pay attention. Assimilation does not engender educational achievement, but access to tribal language and culture for Indian youth does.

How does No Child Left Behind affect Indian country?

All educational institutions in the United States rely heavily on funding from state government. This is true for all public schools, most private schools, and all tribal and charter schools. Without state-supplied per-pupil funding, most schools would not be able to operate. The federal government pressures states with education initiatives such as No Child Left Behind. And state governments in turn keep pressure on school districts to generate educational achievement among their students. Money follows success.

There are many problems with the policy. It holds schools accountable for the achievement of their students at a certain level. It does not matter if the teacher brings a kid from the first-grade reading level to the eleventh-grade reading level. If that kid is in twelfth grade, the teacher still failed. The challenges are pronounced in Indian country, where the educational achievement (opportunity) gap is severe. In some places, tribal youth are failing state tests in English and in math 50 percent of the time. These stats have brought tremendous pressure on many school districts that serve a lot of native youth. Some are in very rural areas. Should the ultimate consequence—closure of the school—occur, most of those children would be looking at a bus ride of an hour and a half in each direction to get to and from school. While accountability is necessary and understandable, the accounting measures should consider not just achievement at a benchmark but progress from one benchmark to another, demographics, and other variables in constructing a fair measure of teacher and school performance.

Brenda Cassellius, the Minnesota commissioner of education, is actively changing this situation in her state, and some others are trying to make similar reforms. But No Child Left Behind has long been pressuring those who educate Indians away from teaching tribal language and culture and toward teaching math and English reading. While those pressures may be slowly shifting, the heightened sense of alienation and distrust in Indian country will take far longer to abate.

Do all Indians have a free ride to college?

Indians do not all have a free ride to college. Most tribes have scholarship programs, usually requiring a high grade point average of successful applicants. Some of those scholarship programs are very well funded, but many others are not. Also, most scholarship benefits are only extended to enrolled members of federally recognized tribes. Considering the many issues with tribal enrollment in the United States (see page 112), there is a great deal of unfairness and discrepancy in scholarship benefits for Indians. Tens of thousands of scholarships are offered across this country for all sorts of reasons, and native scholarships make up their own small part of that number.

Many Americans feel that Indians are somehow financially privileged in the realm of education. Although only a small percentage of Indians obtain significant financial help with college, I believe it would be perfectly fair if all Indians did get a free ride. As a matter of not only historical experience but also direct government policy, many Indian people have been made to suffer. They suffered not just in the nineteenth century during the height of violence; they suffer today. The Indian population is disproportionately unemployed and impoverished. Financial opportunities have been slow in coming to Indian country. Considering all that America does to address poverty throughout the world, including funding the United Nations and the World Bank, it is high time for this country to do more for its Indian citizens. And rather than a handout, I think educational benefits would be perfectly appropriate.

Perspectives: Coming to Terms and Future Directions

> "Nothing can stop an Indian who
> knows who he is."
>
> MARGARET TREUER in *Ojibwe in Minnesota*

Why are Indians so often imagined rather than understood?

Part of the story is simple math. American Indians are a very small percentage of the global population and even a small percentage of the U.S. population. In some parts of the country, one is likely to run into an Indian. But for most Americans, direct contact with an Indian is rare, and a deep conversation with one even more elusive. The situation is very different for many other racial groups in America. African Americans comprise a much larger percentage of the U.S. population. Asians comprise a larger percentage of the U.S. population and a much larger percentage of the world population. The same is true for Spanish-speaking people.

However, there is more to the story than the math. Part of the reason for this lack of understanding about Indians has to do with who controls the story. A great many well-educated African American people in the United States occupy positions of economic and political power. There are many black teachers, Asian teachers, and Hispanic teachers. Surely, there are not enough. But the numbers are still greater than those of Native American teachers. Very few Indians have PhDs and write books. The civil rights movement, for example, brought a great deal of attention to America's unfair treatment of black citizens. Since then, there have been successful efforts to weave strands into the curriculum about black history and black heroes. But there has never been a comparable effort to weave Indian heroes into the curriculum on a system-wide basis. With so few Indians in the world, and so few of them in positions of educational, financial, and political power, prevailing assumptions about Indians often go unchallenged, or the challenges lack efficacy. Indians proliferate as mascots for sport teams when no other racial group in the country is similarly denigrated or mocked (see page 119). Americans are left to their imaginings.

For Indians who do obtain higher education, there is an understandable urge to return to their home communities and serve their own people. Tribal governments and tribal colleges are eager to hire their own. As a result, Indians do their part to maintain their own isolation, even if their actions are not intended to isolate. And that allows people to imagine, rather than to understand through personal experience.

As a white person, I don't feel privileged. So what do Indians mean by that term?

Most white Americans are reluctant to say that they are privileged, even though many may feel and say that people of color in this country are sometimes underprivileged. However, if others around us are less privileged than we are, our status is defined as one of greater privilege. Peggy McIntosh, author of "White Privilege: Unpacking the Invisible Knapsack," and other scholars have done a lot of good writing on this subject.

There are many ways in which white Americans are privileged. Many of those privileges are ones that everybody should enjoy. They include relatively benign things like being able to walk into a store and purchase Band-Aids that more or less match the color of one's skin, or walking into a barbershop or beauty salon knowing that you will find someone who knows how to cut your hair. These are simple, basic privileges that make life easier for whites than for others but are usually taken for granted.

White privileges extend to more serious things, too. A white person who is pulled over by the police can assume that the color of his or her skin was not a factor in being detained, but people of color can never be entirely sure. And people with reservation license plates often wonder if the plates were a factor.[1] Whites also never have to wonder if the color of their skin was part of the process (conscious or not) in banking decisions or loan approvals, but Indians often feel that it is, and historically it has been.[2]

Whites never get asked to speak for all white people. Everyone knows there is a diversity of opinion on any subject, and nobody could speak for all members of their race, but Indians are often asked to speak for or represent their entire race. These are among the types of differential treatments and attitudes that create white privilege.

Why don't tribes solve their own problems?

Tribes are doing more than most people think to address the problems in their communities. They have education, work, health, and poverty programs. They are developing infrastructure and seeking cooperative ventures with state and local governments in spite of the fact that their sovereignty does not require them to do so. Not all tribes have the same resources to work with in creating infrastructure and programs, so they do not develop or heal at the same rate. Some of the tribal efforts have been heroic and truly made positive changes. But problems are so deep and pervasive that it will take years of consistent intervention to really make things better. There is improvement on many fronts, though surely more work needs to be done by tribes. But the rest of America should join that effort as well, and not just because of historical injustices. Indians are Americans too.

All these problems are not my fault. Why should I be asked to atone for the sins of my ancestors?

I once had a conversation with a woman at Princeton University who opposed affirmative action. Her great-great-grandparents were southern plantation slave owners and extremely wealthy. Even after the Civil War, their family retained tremendous wealth and passed it on through generations. When I was talking to this woman, who attended the most prestigious private high school in the country and now one of the best and most expensive universities in the world, I asked how she felt about the fact that her opportunities were purchased with wealth built on the backs of others in slavery. I told her that the direct descendants of the slaves that her great-great-grandparents owned had exactly the opposite experience. Even if they were just as bright and just as deserving of the opportunities and privileges she enjoyed, they were denied access to private schools and universities with high tuitions because of financial barriers. There was probably a host of other barriers to their educational and social advancement as well. How fair was that? I was not of the opinion that she should jump off a bridge to make things right, but I had a hard time reconciling her opposition to affirmative action with her personal history.

On a larger though less obvious level, this is the issue with atonement for the sins of one's ancestors. White people have consistently enjoyed privileges (educational, financial, social, political) that Indians and other people of color have been denied. The world is not a fair place. The past cannot be changed, but many things in the present that are also not fair we can do something about. While it is not fair to hold an individual entirely responsible for the sins of one's ancestors, it is fair to expect our society to remedy the current impact of historical trauma and injustice and inequity. German and Swiss banks had to make reparations to the families of Holocaust victims for the gold fillings extracted from the teeth in their dead bodies and minted into coin. The German government had to make formal apologies for the Final Solution and mandate instruction about the Holocaust in its school systems. All of that makes perfect sense. But here in America, we have yet to get to meaningful formal apologies, much less substantive and comprehensive mandated instruction about genocidal policies toward Indians.

Guilt for whites and anger for Indians are neither healthy nor positive emotions. They are natural emotive responses, but they won't fix anything. The critical challenge of all the troubling history in our country is to turn guilt and anger into positive action. We all need to come to terms with our collective past.

Is there anything wrong with saying that some of my best friends are Indians?

Yes. Some of your best friends might be Indians, but touting that line sounds like you are using your friends to tell the world "see, I'm not racist." It sounds like an effort to alleviate personal guilt or insecurity about race. So, be friends with Indians, but don't use your friendships as a badge or public statement about race.

Is there something wrong with saying that my great-grandmother was a Cherokee princess?

Yes. A large percentage of white and black Americans have native ancestry, and Cherokee is one of the groups widely represented in the gene pool. But the Cherokee did not have kings, queens, princes, or princesses. And saying that "my great-grandmother was a Cherokee princess" makes a profound statement about identity. If your great-grandmother was Cherokee, then one of your grandparents was too, and one of your parents, and in actuality you are Cherokee as well. Someone who truly identifies with his or her native ancestry will say, "I am Cherokee." Everyone understands that at least some of one's ancestors were, too, by that statement.

Claims that "my great-grandmother was a Cherokee princess" usually come from some level of ignorance about Cherokee history and culture, no matter how well intended the statement is. To many Indians, the statement also sounds a lot like claims that "some of my best friends are Indians" (see page 150). To them, it speaks less to one's personal identity and more to one's sense of guilt (or ignorance). It sounds like another way of saying, "See, I'm not racist," rather than a proud statement about heritage. Those who have investigated their heritage would say, "I'm Cherokee," and know that princesses had nothing to do with it.

I might have some Indian ancestry. How do I find out?

A lot of people do have native ancestry. There has been a very high rate of adoption and foster care in native communities, in part orchestrated by missionary organizations and others as part of the larger assimilation initiatives that dominated American Indian policy for decades. Lots of Indians also married outside of their communities, and their descendants absorbed into the general population after a couple of generations. There are also large enclaves of Métis and other mixed Indian-European groups. Some Métis absorbed into the general population in Canada and the United States, some absorbed into tribal populations at Turtle Mountain (North Dakota) and other places, and some maintained distinct communities. The diversity of experiences makes tracking ancestry complicated.

The best thing to do is exhaust one's personal information and archives first. Talk with relatives. Once connection to a specific community can be determined, query those tribes or communities. Many tribes keep large genealogical records for purposes of tribal enrollment and sometimes separate databases for specific land settlements or lawsuits. Those repositories are not often staffed with lots of people to help with generic questions like "Am I Indian?" But if you have the names of specific Indians from those specific communities, they can often help. Check online, as most tribes keep websites and some have moved some records online. Other places to look include the Mormon Church database, which is quite large, ancestry.com, and other research institutions and archives.

Why is that picture *End of the Trail* so popular in Indian country?

I have often wondered the same thing myself. The picture shows a half-naked, feathered Indian slumped over his horse, as if defeated and emotionally devastated. I never identified with that

End of the Trail, original sculpture by James Earl Fraser

image or message. But the artwork became extremely popular in America in the early 1970s.

Dee Brown's famous book, *Bury My Heart at Wounded Knee* (1970), was one of the first published histories that was truly sympathetic to Indians. It covered the most famous stories of Indian military defeat and massacre in the American west. That book, and the statements it quoted from *Black Elk Speaks*, grabbed the attention and inspired the empathy of many Americans about Indian history. Indians were fading into the sunset. And the *End of the Trail* image seemed to capture the popular sentiment well. So it went up on posters and postcards across the country. Why Indians like it so much is still confusing to me. I think Indians were desperate to find something native for their walls, and this image was readily available.

Regarding casinos and treaty rights, I'm not racist, but it doesn't seem fair to me. What's wrong with that line of thinking?

The world is not a fair place. It never has been. But any benefit that any tribe or tribal member gains from casinos or treaty rights pales in comparison to privileges white people enjoy every day in the form of economic, educational, and political opportunity that Indians typically do not receive. And the disadvantages that Indians have growing up in many places where the unemployment rate is 50 percent or higher completely overshadow any advantage that many might receive in the form of different dates for their hunting season. In a couple of Indian communities, casinos have provided a truly outsized benefit for tribal members, but those are the exceptions, not the rule, for 99 percent of the tribal population in America.

In addition to the fairness barometer, the legal underpinnings of treaty rights and Indian law are so deeply embedded in the American legal system that changing the status of tribes as nations or abrogating their treaty rights would involve revisiting the U.S. constitution and the treaties that gave America to nonnative people. The financial and political cost of such an undertaking overwhelms any benefit gained by tribes or their members. Tribal benefits and sovereign status are part of the price America paid for the land.

I'm not racist, but it all happened in the past. Why can't Indians just move on?

Historical trauma is a complicated subject. It's kind of like this. Someone was hitting the Indian in the head with a hammer for decades, and it did a lot of damage. Now the government is (for the most part) done hitting the Indian in the head with a hammer. But there is still all this damage that takes a very long time to repair. And the government is not interested in repairing the damage—it all happened in the past. So Indians are left to heal themselves. Language and culture loss, many health issues, substance abuse, the educational opportunity gap, lack of economic opportunity, and many other problems in Indian country can be directly attributed to specific government policies. It's easy to push people into a pit, but it can be very hard for them to climb back out.

Another way to look at it is this. If a husband cheats on his wife but then decides he wants to reconcile the relationship and make it work, he cannot say, "It all happened in the past. Just forget about it." Making peace has to start with him saying, "Hey, I did you wrong. I am sorry. And it will never happen again." Then there is a chance that they can reconcile the relationship. That is a fair analogy to what happened with the U.S. government and the Indian. Instead of cheating in a marriage, the U.S. government used genocidal warfare, residential boarding schools, suppression of religious freedom, and a host of pernicious policies against Indians. But the government has never even said that it was wrong, much less apologized, much less tried to make things right. And every time the government comes up with a new English-only law, or ignores the 50 percent unemployment rate in some Indian communities, or allows a state like Arizona to ban the teaching of ethnic studies in public schools, or tries to renege on or renegotiate a promised treaty right, Indians see it as another hammer blow to an ancient wound. The historical baggage and the ongoing damage make it very difficult for Indians to move on, discard anger, forgive, or heal. And the fact that most Americans have no understanding of this dynamic makes the struggle all the more frustrating.

Why do Indian people often seem angry?

People in pain are rarely happy, and Indians are in pain. Chronic unemployment and poverty, pervasive substance abuse, and lack of economic and political power plague many native communities. The situation would be bad enough if it were just bad luck or circumstance, but we know that the source of a lot of the problems in Indian country can be traced to specific government actions. The U.S. government carried out a systematic effort to politically and economically disempower Indians and to eradicate Indian culture. Genocidal wars, residential boarding schools, and many other policies did tremendous damage to native communities. That makes people angry.

And many of the most pernicious policies are not so ancient. Circular 1665, which was used to actively suppress tribal religions, was in effect until 1933, within the living memory of many tribal elders today. Most of the grandparent generation carry vivid memories and emotional scars from their experiences at residential boarding schools run by the U.S. government. Anger from such experiences does not fade overnight. And on top of it all, most American people do not understand Indians or their experiences very well. The curriculum in most schools still gives candy-coated versions of Christopher Columbus and Thanksgiving, when Indians know the history was far different from what is often taught (see pages 25, 34). Being imagined and misunderstood breeds anger, too.

Anger is not a healthy emotion. Many native people challenge themselves and others to convert that understandable feeling into positive action, but there is not always much help from the outside. Curriculum reform is slow and often resisted. Politicians are more likely to pass a bill requiring that English be declared the official language than to support tribal language and culture revitalization. All of that serves to stir up the hornet's nest. It's an uphill battle.

Do Indians ever work together?

Yes, Indians work together, and sometimes with great positive effect. There are national and international indigenous organizations tackling issues from environmental protection to political and economic reform. At the tribal and grassroots level, there have been many efforts to address health, education, economics, and language and culture revitalization. Some have been incredibly inspiring.

What are some good books to read about Indians?

Many great books, documentary videos, and websites have been produced in recent years, and I've listed some suggestions for further reading at the back of this book. There are several things to remember as you read. Writers of all races and genders have points of view, so you have to be alert and understand that when you see it. You can't judge the accuracy or authenticity of a book by the race of its author. Indian writers can get it wrong; non-Indian writers can get it wrong. Both can get it beautifully right. And it may sound odd to say it, but also keep in mind that even the most authentic works of fiction are not history.

Are there any good Indian movies?

I like some of the old spaghetti westerns because the Navajo extras they hired spent the entire time talking smack about the actors in the Diné language. With proper translation, it's incredibly entertaining. Hollywood has a really hard time getting away from creating a white character who is better than the Indian at being Indian, like Kevin Costner in *Dances with Wolves*. A lot of Indians loved that movie, by the way, simply because the Indians didn't all die and a lot of native actors played parts. Many Indians favor independent films like *Dance Me Outside*, *Powwow Highway*, and *Smoke Signals*. But movies are entertainment, and if you want genuine understanding, the list of documentaries and published works in the back of this book is a better place to look.

Have you ever been the object of direct racial discrimination?

My experiences are like those of many other Indians, but the pain at the time was all my own. In first grade, I had long hair, and my teacher dressed me up like a girl in front of the entire class, complete with barrettes and makeup. She and everyone else in class had a good laugh at my expense. It was completely humiliating. When I was in seventh grade, I sat in shop class with three nonnative kids who were horribly, deliberately racist. They spent the entire class saying that Indians were all drunks and I would be a drunk too, that Indians were a disgrace and shouldn't be allowed to live in America, that Indians were all on welfare and sucking the country dry, that Indians were responsible for all the crime in the area, and that tribal governments designed license plates with numbers that were hard for cops to read so Indian criminals could escape. I told them they were wrong, but they insisted that their parents told them it was true and I was wrong because I was a dumb Indian. I confronted one of the kids before school, telling him it had to stop. He pounded my lips onto my braces, and the comments and snickers continued for the rest of the quarter. Usually racism is subtle, but these encounters with its overt forms left some very deep scars.

I also experienced forms of racism so common they are clichés. As a teenager and as an adult, I was sometimes followed around stores by clerks who apparently thought I was likely to shoplift because I am identifiably native. A couple of times when I was shopping, the clerk at the checkout asked me to present my EBT card (food stamps), apparently assuming that all Indians paid for their groceries that way.

You're a testament to your race. How did you turn out so good?

Be careful. For one thing, I'm really not that good. But more important, stereotyping is highly problematic, and you can never judge an entire race of people by the actions of one person. A statement like the one above suggests a negative stereotype of Indians—that a good Indian is atypical. Indians are diverse and complicated. Not all white people are the same, and not all whites have the same beliefs. It's the same for Indians.

How can I learn more?

In addition to consulting the list of resources in the back of this book, I encourage people to open their minds and hearts. Seek out Indians for answers about Indians. Attend a powwow. Go to a tribal language table. Join your area race relations task force. It always amazes me how many of the books and resources about Indians had no input from Indians. Tribes and tribal people are getting better at reaching out and developing more resources online and in print. Seek out those things, and don't be discouraged. There are still a lot of Indians who are understandably angry about a lot of things, and they can be discouraging to others, even those engaged in a genuine quest for understanding and a desire to help. But it is only through the combined efforts of a great many native and nonnative people that we will make it easier for Indians to be understood rather than imagined.

Conclusion:
Finding Ways to Make
a Difference

"All that is necessary for evil to triumph
is for good men to do nothing."
EDMUND BURKE

How can I help?

Sometimes the brambled racial borderland of my youth seems
as impenetrable as it ever was. Indians remain imagined more
than they are understood. Public and political backlash against
Indian casinos and treaty rights is still obvious. Indians are still
often used as mascots for sports teams, with broad resistance
to change or a lack of understanding of the impact of that resistance on native people. Problems persist in Indian country, and
with the types of drugs and ease of access found in the modern
world, things like substance abuse seem even worse.

But looks can be deceiving. Last spring I brought my van to
Kenny's Clark Station in Bemidji, Minnesota, to get new tires. I
have known the owners, the Merschmans, most of my life, and
I like to support family businesses in our area. They have always been kind and respectful to me, and they know how to fix
cars. Paying for new tires is a painful experience for a penny-
pincher like me, but I was amazed when I settled my bill to hear
owner Alan Merschman tell me, "Miigwech. Giga-waabamin
miinawaa." My white mechanic spoke to me in the Ojibwe lan-

guage. My language. This had never happened to me before. And this would not have been possible just a few years earlier. Something was changing in the borderland.

I live near the town of Bemidji in northern Minnesota, right between the three largest Indian reservations in the state. About a third of the population there is native, but about half of the shopping population is native. Bemidji was not always a friendly place for Indians. In 1967, local resort owner and Beltrami County commissioner Robert Kohl gave a live radio broadcast on KBUN in which he went on a racial rant, declaring that Indians were all drunks and leeches on the government. Kohl said that Indians "are so low on the human scale that it is doubtful they will ever climb upward . . . Perhaps we should have let nature take her course, let disease and malnutrition disrupt the reproductive process and weed out those at the very bottom of the heap."[1] The fact that Indians did half of the shopping in Bemidji and had none of the jobs was hard enough, but this was intolerable.

Red Lake tribal chairman Roger Jourdain led a boycott of Bemidji area businesses in 1967, soon joined by Leech Lake and White Earth. The Bemidji Area Chamber of Commerce tried to apologize on Robert Kohl's behalf, but the boycott continued until Kohl himself apologized. Realizing the importance of his native patrons, Joseph Lueken, owner of the local grocery chain, instituted an affirmative action employment policy after the boycott as well.[2]

The boycott was a big step forward in my community, but the Indian and non-Indian worlds still rarely interacted unless they had to. When interactions were unavoidable, they were often negative. Indians had to deal with nonnative police, lawyers, judges, teachers, and bankers. They often perceived their treatment to be racially biased. Some of that perception was based on a misplaced assumption that all nonnative people in positions of educational, political, and financial power were prejudiced against Indians (because so many of them had been in the past). But some of that perception was accurate. Independent studies of law enforcement in Bemidji have indicated a real issue with racial profiling in particular.³ Many white educators, bankers, and lawyers had negative attitudes about Indians, but many more wanted to get along with Native Americans. However, they were so terrified of offending angry Indians that they found it safer not to teach about them or take perceived risks by doing business with them.

How did we get from that dynamic to Alan Merschman engaging me in my tribal language with no outside pressure or formal training? Enter Michael Meuers, Rachelle Houle, and Noemi Ayelsworth. Together, these three nonnative people envisioned and carried out an ambitious

Alan Merschman, owner of Kenny's Clark Station in Bemidji, Minnesota

A grassroots effort in Bemidji, Minnesota, started by Michael Meuers has succeeded in convincing most area businesses to post their signs bilingually in Ojibwe and English.

initiative as part of Bemidji's anti-racism organization, Shared Vision. Michael Meuers was the primary advocate for tribal language proliferation in Bemidji. He wanted welcome signs for local businesses and informational signs about bathrooms to be presented bilingually in the local tribal language (Ojibwe) and in English. When you travel to Hawaii, everyone knows what *aloha* means, and everyone in northern Minnesota should know what *boozhoo* means. Local heritage and language is part of what makes every place special. The idea of bilingual signage was also to present nonnative storeowners with a safe way to reach out to Indian communities around Bemidji. Rachelle Houle joined him, going door to door to convince area businesses to post their signs bilingually. Noemi Ayelsworth, owner of the Cabin Coffee House, was the first businessperson to post bilingual signs and join the effort.

Soon, Eugene Stillday, a tribal elder and fluent speaker from Ponemah on the Red Lake Reservation, and I joined a list of resource people to translate phrases, words, and signs. I worked with fellow staff at Bemidji State University to develop instructional materials for free access online (see www.bemidjistate .edu/airc). With no money, this grassroots effort soon convinced over 120 area businesses to put up their signs bilingually in Ojibwe and English, and the initiative continues to grow. The university, hospital, area schools, and regional events center all have bilingual signs, and Ojibwe language is proliferating throughout the community. It is now common to hear cashiers at Target engage tribal elders in Ojibwe. Alan Merschman is not alone. Indians feel welcomed in places where they never did before. Shop owners feel there is a safe way to reach out to native clientele. Bilingual signage does not solve all the big problems. But it does enlarge the safe space in which we can all talk about those big problems, and that's a huge start. And that huge start began through the advocacy of three nonnative people.

There are many ways to get involved. In Hawaii, a grassroots language revitalization effort pushed the number of fluent speakers from five hundred to around twelve thousand, and a significant number of those speakers are not even Hawaiian. Most were working in schools with Native Hawaiians and picked up the language as part of the effort to preserve and revitalize native culture and language. Their involvement has been welcomed. In economic development, political networking and advocacy, education, health care, and many other fields, there is a role for native and nonnative people. Indians are a tiny percentage of the population in this country, but in Minnesota and many other places they comprise 20 percent of the homeless population. We need help with everything from education to grant writing to advocacy. If you are not part of the solution, you might be part of the problem. Teachers too afraid to teach about Indians are likely perpetuating stereotypes of Indians or erroneous versions of the Christopher Columbus story, alienating Indians without even realizing they are doing it.

It can be very frustrating for nonnative people to know how best to reach out to Indians or to help address the problems in Indian country. Most human beings are terrified of offend-

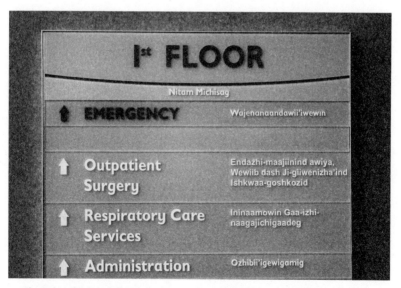

The university, hospital, event center, and public schools in Bemidji, Minnesota, have posted bilingual signs.

ing others or being accused of racism. Sometimes it seems safer and easier not to teach about Indians, not to learn more and more deeply about Indians, and not to advocate for change. But Edmund Burke had it right: "All that is necessary for evil to triumph is for good men to do nothing." So don't imagine Indians, understand them. Keep asking questions, reading, listening, and advocating for change. Don't tolerate stereotypes, and don't be afraid to ask everything you wanted to know about Indians. And if you're native, give a meaningful response to those questions rather than an angry rebuke. It really does make a difference. In the words of my white mechanic, Alan Merschman, "Miigwech. Giga-waabamin miinawaa."[4]

Acknowledgments

My time devoted to this project was in part enabled by support from the American Philosophical Society, the Bush Leadership Fellows Program, and the John Simon Guggenheim Foundation.

Thank you to Michael Meuers for suggesting the title for this book and the lecture series that inspired it and for his leadership in promoting bilingual signage in Bemidji along with Rachelle Houle and Noemi Ayelsworth. Thanks also to Rose Jones, whose advocacy helped make the development of free online Ojibwe resource material a reality. Thank you to those who shared the podium with me for some of the "Everything You Ever Wanted to Know" events, including Donald Day, Benjamin Burgess, Renee Gurneau, Michael Gonzales, and Minnie Oakgrove. I am also deeply indebted to Rose Tainter, Thelma Nayquonabe, Monique Paulson, Lisa LaRonge, Lisa Clemens, Alex Decoteau, Cathy Begay, and Michelle Haskins for assistance with cultural information included in this work. Thank you to Andrew Wickert for fact-checking the section on Clovis. Thanks to Jill Doerfler and David Treuer for feedback on enrollment. Miigwech to Gerald Auginash and Michael Meuers for help with pictures. The text for this book was graced by the fine editorial scrutiny of Cary Miller, Ann Regan, and Shannon Pennefeather, all of whom made it better.

I received lots of support while writing this book and traveling on the lecture series that inspired it. Special thanks to Alfred Bush, Thomas Stillday, Anna Gibbs, Eugene Stillday, Archie Mosay, Dora Ammann, Brooke Ammann, Sean Fahrlander, Keller Paap, Lisa LaRonge, Rick and Penny Kagigebi, Isadore Toulouse, Daniel and Gail Jones, Dennis Jones, Dustin Burnette,

Charles Grolla, James Hardy, Adrian Liberty, Henry Flocken, Diane Amour, Donna Beckstrom, David Thorstad, Donovan Sather, Jordyn Flaada, Paul and Betty Day, Donald and Priscilla Day, Benjamin and Tahnee Burgess, Collette Dahlke, Stephanie Hendricks, Thomas Goldtooth, Ted Waukey, Leon Valliere, Linda Wade, Irene Benjamin, Skip and Babette Sandman, Leonard and Mary Moose, Michael and Krysten Sullivan, Michael, Midge, Frank, and Mark Montano, Joan Poor, Dick Hanson, and Nancy Erickson.

I have a large and incredible family that has been my greatest strength in all that I do. I am especially indebted to my parents Robert and Margaret Treuer, my siblings Smith, Paul, Derek, Megan, Micah, and David Treuer, and their spouses. My children have been forced to share me with the rest of the world because of my ceremonial obligations and academic work. Their generosity always amazes me. Thank you to Jordan, Robert, Madeline, Caleb, Isaac, Elias, Evan, Mia, and Luella. My wife, Blair Treuer, really deserves to have her name on the cover of every book I write because she gives so much to the effort. I could never say thank you enough to show my real appreciation.

Recommended Reading

Tribal Language and Culture

Broker, Ignatia. *Night Flying Woman: An Ojibway Narrative.* St. Paul: Minnesota Historical Society Press, 1983.

Hinton, Leann. *How to Keep Your Language Alive.* Berkeley, CA: Heyday Books, 2002.

Johnston, Basil. *Ojibway Heritage.* Lincoln: University of Nebraska Press, 1990.

Kegg, Maude. *Portage Lake: Memories of an Ojibwe Childhood.* Minneapolis: University of Minnesota Press, 1991.

Moose, Lawrence L., et al. *Aaniin Ekidong: Ojibwe Vocabulary Project.* St. Paul: Minnesota Humanities Center, 2009.

Nichols, John D., and Earl Nyholm (Otchingwanigan). *A Concise Dictionary of Minnesota Ojibwe.* Minneapolis: University of Minnesota Press, 1995.

Treuer, Anton. *Living Our Language: Ojibwe Tales and Oral Histories.* St. Paul: Minnesota Historical Society Press, 2001.

Early History

Blackhawk, Ned. *Violence over the Land.* Cambridge, MA: Harvard University Press, 2006.

Brown, Dee. *Bury My Heart at Wounded Knee.* New York: Holt, Rinehart & Winston, 1970.

Copway, George. *The Traditional History and Characteristic Sketches of the Ojibway Nation.* London: Charles Gilpin, 1850. Reprinted in the United States as *Indian Life and Indian History, by an Indian Author: Embracing the Traditions of the North American Indians Regarding Themselves, Particularly of*

That Most Important of All the Tribes, the Ojibways. Boston: Albert Cosby and Company, 1858.

Josephy, Alvin. *500 Nations*. New York: Pimlico, 2005.

Koning, Hans. *Columbus: His Enterprise*. New York: Monthly Review Press, 1991.

Kugel, Rebecca. *To Be the Main Leaders of Our People: A History of Minnesota Ojibwe Politics, 1825–1898*. East Lansing: Michigan State University Press, 1998.

Mann, Charles. *1491: New Revelations of the Americas before Columbus*. New York: Knopf, 2005.

Meyer, Melissa. *The White Earth Tragedy: Ethnicity and Dispossession at a Minnesota Anishinaabe Reservation*. Lincoln: University of Nebraska Press, 1994.

Miller, Cary. *Ogimaag: Anishinaabeg Leadership, 1760–1845*. Lincoln: University of Nebraska Press, 2010.

Rethinking Columbus. Milwaukee, WI: Rethinking Schools, 1991.

Schenck, Theresa. *The Voice of the Crane Echoes Afar: The Sociopolitical Organization of the Lake Superior Ojibwa, 1640–1855*. New York: Garland, 1997.

Tanner, Helen Hornbeck, ed. *Atlas of Great Lakes Indian History*. Norman: University of Oklahoma Press, 1987.

Treuer, Anton. *The Assassination of Hole in the Day*. St. Paul, MN: Borealis Books, 2011.

Warren, William W. *History of the Ojibway People*. St. Paul: Minnesota Historical Society Press, 1984. Originally published as *History of the Ojibways Based upon Traditions and Oral Statements* (1885).

Legal History

Duthu, N. Bruce. *American Indians and the Law*. London: Penguin Books, 2008.

Getches, David H., and Charles F. Wilkinson. *Federal Indian Law: Cases and Materials*. St. Paul, MN: West Publishing, 1986.

Wilkins, David. *American Indian Sovereignty and the U.S. Supreme Court: The Masking of Justice*. Austin: University of Texas Press, 1997.

Contemporary History and Government Indian Policy

Adams, David Wallace. *Education for Extinction: American Indians and the Boarding School Experience, 1875–1928*. Lawrence: University Press of Kansas, 1995.

Child, Brenda. *Boarding School Seasons: American Indian Families, 1900–1940*. Lincoln: University of Nebraska Press, 1998.

Fixico, Donald L. *Termination and Relocation: Federal Indian Policy, 1945–1960*. Albuquerque: University of New Mexico Press, 1986.

Graves, Kathy David, and Elizabeth Ebbott. *Indians in Minnesota*. Minneapolis: University of Minnesota Press, 2006.

Hoxie, Frederick. *A Final Promise: The Campaign to Assimilate the Indians, 1880–1920*. New York: Routledge, 2001.

Olson, James, and Raymond Wilson. *Native Americans in the Twentieth Century*. Urbana: University of Illinois Press, 1986.

Prucha, Francis Paul. *The Great Father: The United States Government and the American Indian*. Lincoln: University of Nebraska Press, 1986.

Russell, Steve. *Sequoyah Rising: Problems in Post-Colonial Tribal Governance*. Raleigh, NC: Carolina Academic Press, 2010.

Treuer, Anton. *Ojibwe in Minnesota*. St. Paul: Minnesota Historical Society Press, 2010.

Perspectives and Philosophy

Berkhofer, Robert. *The White Man's Indian*. New York: Knopf, 1978.

Deloria, Philip. *Playing Indian*. New Haven, CT: Yale University Press, 1998.

Deloria, Vine Jr. *Custer Died for Your Sins: An Indian Manifesto*. New York: Macmillan, 1969.

Deloria, Vine Jr. *Red Earth, White Lies: Native Americans and the Myth of Scientific Fact.* New York: Scribner, 1995.

Lyons, Scott. *X-Marks: Native Signatures of Assent.* Minneapolis: University of Minnesota Press, 2010.

Neihardt, John G. *Black Elk Speaks.* Lincoln: University of Nebraska Press, 1979.

Russell, Steve. *Sequoyah Rising: Problems in Post-Colonial Tribal Governance.* Durham, NC: Carolina Academic Press, 2010.

Weatherford, Jack. *Native Roots: How the Indians Enriched America.* New York: Fawcett Columbine, 1991.

Literature

Alexie, Sherman. *Reservation Blues.* New York: Atlantic Monthly, 1995.

Erdrich, Louise. *Tracks.* New York: Harper Collins, 1988.

Momaday, N. Scott. *House Made of Dawn.* New York: Harper Collins, 1966.

Silko, Leslie Marmon. *Ceremony.* New York: Penguin, 2006.

Treuer, David. *The Translation of Dr. Appelles.* New York: Random House, 2008.

Video Documentaries

500 Nations (1995)

The Dakota Conflict (1993)

First Speakers: Restoring the Ojibwe Language (2010)

Geronimo and the Apache Resistance (2007)

Incident at Oglala (2004)

Lighting the 7th Fire (1995)

Waasa Inaabidaa (2002)

We Shall Remain (2010)

Woodlands: Story of the Mille Lacs Ojibwe (1994)

Notes

Notes to "Terminology"

1. There are no such references in Columbus's journals or letters. David Wilton did a good job exposing the untruth of this assertion in *Word Myths: Debunking Linguistic Urban Legends* (New York: Oxford University Press, 2009).
2. Sherman Alexie, reading, Schwartz Books, Milwaukee, Wisconsin, Mar. 1993.
3. Ives Goddard in *News From Indian Country* (mid-Apr. 1997).
4. The Forest County Potawatomi (Wisconsin) and the Citizen Band Potawatomi (Kansas) prefer *Potawatomi* to other spellings. Billy Daniels, Forest County Potawatomi elder, affirmed this spelling when I interviewed him. The Ho-Chunk Nation of Wisconsin prefers *Ho-Chunk* to the commonly used term *Winnebago*. The Assiniboine of Fort Belknap prefer *Assiniboine* to its numerous alternate spellings. The Menominee of Wisconsin prefer *Menominee* to the published alternatives. The Grand Traverse Band (Michigan) and Oklahoma Band of Ottawa (Oklahoma) both prefer *Ottawa* to the other versions of their name.

Notes to "History"

1. James Adovasio and Jake Page, *The First Americans: In Pursuit of Archaeology's Greatest Mystery* (New York: Random House, 2003); N. Guidon and G. Delibrias, "Carbon-14 Dates Point to Man in the Americas 32,000 Years Ago," *Nature* 321 (1986): 769–71; Robson Bonnichsen and Karen L. Turnmire, *Clovis: Origins and Adaptations* (Corvallis: Oregon State University Press, 1991); Mary C. Stiner, "Modern Human Origins—Faunal Perspectives," *Annual Review of Anthropology* (1993): 55–77; David Hurst Thomas, *Exploring Ancient Native America: An Archaeological Guide* (New York: Macmillan, 1994); David S. Whitley and Ronald I. Dorn, "New Perspectives on the Clovis vs. Pre-Clovis Controversy," *American Antiquity* 58.4 (1993): 626–47; John Noble Wilford, "Support for Early Date of Arrival in America," *New York Times*, Feb. 1, 1994; Charles C. Mann, *1491: New Revelations of the Americas before Columbus* (New York: Random House, 2005).

Other sites under current excavation and investigation that challenge the Clovis First Theory include Channel Islands (California), Leech Lake (Walker, Minnesota), Big Eddy (Missouri), Page-Ladson (Jefferson County, Florida), Mud Lake and Schaefer-Hebior Mammoth (Kenosha County, Wisconsin), Paisley Caves (Oregon), Cactus Hill (Virginia), Tlapacoya (Lake Chalco Pedra Furada, Serra da Capivara National Park, Brazil), Lagoa Santa (Minas Gerais, Brazil), Cueva Fell and Pali Aike Crater (Patagonia), and Taima Taima (Venezuela).

2. George Catlin, *Letters and Notes on the Manners, Customs, and Conditions of North American Indians*, 2 vols. (New York: Dover Publications, 1973), 1:238–40; Frances Densmore, *Chippewa Customs* (St. Paul: Minnesota Historical Society Press, 1979), 135; George W. Featherstonhaugh, *A Canoe Voyage up the Minnay Sotor with an Account of the Lead and Copper Deposits in Wisconsin; of the Gold Region in the Cherokee Country; and Sketches of Popular Manners* (St. Paul: Minnesota Historical Society Press, 1970), 1:362–63; Basil Johnston, *Ojibway Ceremonies* (Lincoln: University of Nebraska Press, 1990), 75–76; Edmund Jefferson Danziger, Jr., *The Chippewas of Lake Superior* (Norman: University of Oklahoma Press, 1979), 24–25; Henry Lewis, *The Valley of the Mississippi Illustrated*, trans. Hermina Poatgieter (St. Paul: Minnesota Historical Society Press, 1967), 173–75; and Samuel W. Pond, *The Dakota or Sioux in Minnesota: As They Were in 1834* (St. Paul: Minnesota Historical Society Press, 1986), 130–31; Henry H. Sibley, "Memoir of Jean Nicollet," *Collections of the Minnesota Historical Society* 1 (1902):224; James H. Howard, *The Plains-Ojibwa or Bungi*, Reprints in Anthropology 7 (Vermillion: University of South Dakota Press, 1977), 104; Mary Eastman, *Dahcotah; or Life and Legends of the Sioux around Fort Snelling* (Minneapolis, MN: Ross and Haines, 1962), xx.

3. Frederic Baraga, *Chippewa Indians in 1847* (New York: Studia Slovenica, 1976), 45.

4. Interviews, Earl Otchingwanigan (Nyholm), 1992; Mary Roberts, 1988, 1989; Archie Mosay, 1993; Dora Ammann, 1994; Thomas J. Stillday, 1995; Anna Gibbs, 1998. See also Erwin F. Mittleholtz and Rose Graves, *Historical Review of the Red Lake Indian Reservation: Centennial Souvenir Commemorating a Century of Progress, 1858–1958* (Bemidji, MN: Council of the Red Lake Band of Chippewa Indians and the Beltrami County Historical Society, 1957), 136; Martha Coleman Bray, *The Journals of Joseph N. Nicollet: A Scientist on the Mississippi Headwaters with Notes on Indian Life, 1836–37*, trans. André Fertey (St. Paul: Minnesota Historical Society Press, 1970), 165, 199–211; Walter Williams, *The Spirit and the Flesh: Sexual Diversity in American Indian Culture* (Boston: Beacon Press, 1992), 67–68, 110, 167–68; Alexander Henry and David Thompson, *New Light on the Early History of the Greater Northwest*, ed. Elliott Coues (New York: Harper, 1897), 1:163–65; Louise Phelps Kellogg, *Early Narratives of the Northwest, 1634–1699* (New York: Charles

Scribner's Sons, 1917), 244n; Vernon W. Kinietz, *Chippewa Village* (Bloomfield, MI: Cranbrook Press, 1947), 155; Peter Grant, "The Saulteux Indians about 1804," in *Les Bourgeois de la Compagnie du Nord-Ouest*, ed. L. R. Masson (Quebec City: Imprimerie, 1890), 2:357; Catlin, *Letters and Notes*, 2:214–15; Reuben Gold Thwaites, ed., *The Jesuit Relations and Allied Documents*, 73 vols. (New York: Pageant Book Company, 1959), 59:129, 310; Edwin James, ed., *A Narrative of the Captivity and Adventures of John Tanner during Thirty Years Residence among the Indians in the Interior of North America* (London: Carvill, 1830; reprint, Minneapolis, MN: Ross and Haines, 1956), 105–6; Densmore, *Chippewa Customs*, 87–89; John Parker, ed., *The Journals of Jonathan Carver and Related Documents* (St. Paul: Minnesota Historical Society Press, 1976), 108–10; William W. Warren, *History of the Ojibway People* (St. Paul: Minnesota Historical Society Press, 1984), 264; Pond, *The Dakota or Sioux in Minnesota*, 93–96, 124. An excellent secondary account is discussed in Rebecca Kugel, *To Be the Main Leaders of Our People: A History of Minnesota Ojibwe Politics* (East Lansing: Michigan State University Press, 1998), 71–73, 92n.

5. Interview, Mary Roberts, 1988.

6. I prefer the term "educational opportunity gap" over "achievement gap" but want to avoid confusion here.

7. Christopher Columbus, *The Four Voyages: Being His Own Log-Book, Letters and Dispatches with Connecting Narratives* (New York: Penguin, 1985).

8. Bartolomé de Las Casas, *Brief Account of the Devastation of the Indies* (1542).

9. Bartolomé de Las Casas, *History of the Indies* (1552), as cited in Alvin Josephy, Jr., *500 Nations* (New York: Knopf, 1994), 114.

10. The State of Wisconsin passed ACT 31, which mandates all certified K–12 educators take a class on Indian history or culture, but the requirement is easily satisfied with a weekend workshop. Some public officials have also issued apologies, but here too the efforts have been small, scattershot, and largely unsupported by either the government or the general population.

11. The Minnesota state seal has a very similar image: a white farmer plowing the land as a symbol of progress, with an Indian riding into the sunset. The caption, in French, reads: "L' Étoile du Nord (The Star of the North)."

12. The Powhatan were a confederacy of thirty Algonquian tribes in Virginia in the sixteenth and seventeenth centuries. The term *Powhatan* has been used to refer to the largest tribe in the confederacy, the people of all tribes from the confederacy, the principal village in the confederacy, and its primary chief. Confederacy nations include the Powhatans, Arrohatecks, Appamattucks, Pamunkey, Mattaponis, Chiskiacks, Kecoughtans, Youghtanunds, Rappahannocks,

Moraughtacunds, Weyanoaks, Paspaheghs, Quiyoughcohannocks, and Nansemonds.

13. Anton Treuer, *Ojibwe in Minnesota* (St. Paul: Minnesota Historical Society Press, 2010), 35; Jill St. Germain, *Indian Treaty-Making Policy in the United States and Canada, 1867–1877* (Lincoln: University of Nebraska Press, 2001). The decision to end treaty making with Indian tribes in 1871 was only possible when Indian nations could be treated as subjects of American policy rather than as independent nations.

14. Webster's Online Dictionary, 2011.

15. Article 2, Convention on the Prevention and Punishment of the Crime of Genocide, United Nations, Dec. 9, 1948. Text available at http://www.hrweb.org/legal/genocide.html.

16. Lord Jeffrey Amherst, Commander of British North America Forces, to Colonel Henry Bouquet, July 16, 1763. The letter was authenticated by Francis Parkman, and discussion of it is available at http://www.straightdope.com/columns/read/1088/did-whites-ever-give-native-americans-blankets-infected-with-smallpox.

17. Alexandra Pierce, "Shattered Hearts," report compiled for Minnesota Indian Women's Resource Center (Aug. 2009), 11.

Notes to "Religion, Culture & Identity"

1. Interview, Billy Daniels, Potawatomi elder (1996).

2. Interview, Thomas Stillday (2006).

3. "State Urges Denial of New Trial Bid in Sweat Lodge Case," *Bemidji Pioneer*, July 26, 2011, 12.

4. For a copy of the Code of Indian Offenses, see http://tribal-law.blogspot.com/2008/02/code-of-indian-offenses.html.

Note to "Powwow"

1. There are a few scattered references to "powwow" as old as the late nineteenth century, but they are actually references to ceremonial Big Drum dances rather than to powwows as they are performed and understood today. Modern powwow culture first emerged around World War II, and its current contest configurations developed in the 1970s.

Note to "Tribal Languages"

1. Mii o'ow gidinwewininaan. Mii ow memadweyaashkaagin zaaga'iganiin miinawaa sa go gaye minweweyaandagaasing miinawaa sa go gaye minwewebagaasing ani-dagwaaging. Mii o'ow enitaagoziwaad bineshiinyag nagamotaadiwaad megwayaak miin-

awaa go ma'iinganag waawoonowaad, naawewidamowaad. Mii ow
gidinwewininaan wendinigeyang bimaadiziwin, gikenindizoyang
anishinaabewiyang, gidinwewininaan gechitwaawendaagwak gaa-
ina'oonigooyang gimanidoominaan.

Notes to "Politics"

1. The Oneida case was dismissed by the Second Circuit Court of Appeals in May 2011 but is being appealed to the U.S. Supreme Court:
   Caitlin Traynor, "Oneida Indian Nation Appeals Land Claim Dismissal," *The Oneida Daily Dispatch*, May 24, 2011.
2. Ada Deer as cited in Treuer, *Ojibwe in Minnesota*, 48.
3. The total number of terminated tribal governments is 109, including California Rancherias and Oregon tribal communities covered
   in blanket termination policies and individual termination acts
   from 1953 to 1964. There are additional native groups like the Lum-
   bee that seek official federal recognition but lack a treaty-based
   government-to-government history with the United States since
   most are located on the East Coast, where they had relations with
   the British but lost most of their land before the U.S. government
   came into existence.
4. Public Law 280, Act of Aug. 15, 1953, ch. 505, 67 Stat. 588. For background on and legal challenges to Public Law 280, see Kevin K.
   Washburn, "The Legacy of *Bryan v. Itasca County*: How a $147 County
   Tax Notice Helped Bring Tribes $200 Billion in Indian Gaming Rev-
   enue," *Minnesota Law Review* (forthcoming), available at http://ssrn.
   com/abstract=1008585.
5. *Bryan v. Itasca County* (426 U.S. 373, 1976). In *State of Minnesota v. Stone*
   and *State of Minnesota v. Jackson,* the Minnesota Supreme Court ruled
   that the state could not regulate most traffic laws on reservations
   for Indian defendants.
6. Kathy Graves and Elizabeth Ebbott, *Indians in Minnesota* (Minneapolis: University of Minnesota Press, 2006), 284–85; *Minnesota
   Statewide Racial Profiling Report: Beltrami County Sheriff's Department,*
   report to Minnesota State Legislature by the Institute on Race and
   Poverty, Sept. 23, 2003; Chris Williams, "In Minnesota, Claims of Racial Profiling Indians," *News From Indian Country* (2002).
7. Information on AIM activism is taken from Paul Smith and Robert
   Warrior, *Like a Hurricane: The American Indian Movement from Alcatraz
   to Wounded Knee* (New York: W. W. Norton, 1996).
8. Information on these AIM activities is taken primarily from "Con-
   cerned Indian Americans," charter statement; interview, Clyde Bellecourt, 1994; Russell Means, *Where White Men Fear to Tread* (New
   York: St. Martin's Press, 1995).

9. All of the statistics on adoption and foster care of native children, including the Minnesota-specific figures, are taken from expert testimony on the bill Public Law 95–608 (Indian Child Welfare Act), 9–10, 336–37. Information on impacts of the act and caseload numbers is taken from Graves and Ebbott, *Indians in Minnesota*, 227, 238.

10. Graves and Ebbott, *Indians in Minnesota*, 91.

11. James Dao, "In California, Indian Tribes with Casino Money Cast Off Members," *New York Times*, Dec. 12, 2011. Michigan and other states have seen many tribal members removed from the rolls in recent years as well. Disenrollment usually has less to do with blood quantum than it does with political infighting or per capita payments.

12. Information on tribal enrollment at White Earth and the Jenks and Hrdlicka tests is taken from Records of the United States, Records of the U.S. Attorney, U.S. Department of Justice, "Land Allotment Fraud Cases at White Earth, Deposition Testimony," National Archives, Chicago Regional Branch, 11; Ales Hrdlicka, "Anthropology of the Chippewa," *Holes Anniversary Volume: Anthropological Essays* (Washington, DC: 1916), 198–227; Albert Jenks to William Folwell, May 21, 1926, William Watts Folwell Papers, Minnesota Historical Society, St. Paul; "Professor Jenks Returns to the University," *University of Minnesota Alumni Weekly* 15.21 (Feb. 21, 1916), 12; Ranson J. Powell to Albert Jenks, Nov. 16, 1914, Powell Papers, Minnesota Historical Society, St. Paul; "Popular Picture of Indian Upset by Investigation, Eagle Beak Nose Belongs Not to Red Man, but to Fiction," *Minneapolis Journal*, Apr. 9, 1916, 3; *Minneapolis Journal*, May 1 and 5, 1918, 12; *Minneapolis Tribune*, Nov. 1 and 13, 1920. For reliable secondary sources, see the fantastic article on the eugenics testing and compilation of blood quantum records at White Earth by David L. Beaulieu, "Curly Hair and Big Feet: Physical Anthropology and the Implementation of Land Allotment on the White Earth Chippewa Reservation," *American Indian Quarterly* (Fall 1984): 281–314. See also William W. Folwell, *A History of Minnesota* (St. Paul: Minnesota Historical Society Press, 1956), 4:291–93.

13. White Earth is trying to change the criteria for enrollment, but absent approval from the Bureau of Indian Affairs and the Minnesota Chippewa Tribe, it has been unsuccessful to date.

14. "Of Blood and Citizenship," *Indian Country Today*, July 27, 2011, 27.

15. It is a mutually beneficial proposition. More people would be eligible for help from the tribes, yes, but expanding tribal membership would also help the tribes have larger pools of voters, tribal political leaders, advocates, and educators. Waning membership means waning political power. Italy and Japan, for example, have declined in military and diplomatic position in part because of lower birth rates relative to those of other countries.

16. Diane Wilson's *Beloved Child* (St. Paul, MN: Borealis Books, 2011) provides some great anecdotal examples of this dynamic.
17. Chris Williams, "Suit Calls School's 'Wigger Day' Racist," *St. Paul Pioneer Press,* Aug. 5, 2011, B1.
18. Interview, Sean Fahrlander, Sept. 2009. Fahrlander placed the emphasis on *land,* to clarify that he was serving his people and his place, not the U.S. flag. He also added, "Things were so bad on the reservation that what we were going to was no worse than what we were coming from."

Notes to "Economics"

1. Graves and Ebbott, *Indians in Minnesota,* 95. This data is for the enrolled tribal population. The number of self-identified Indians living on a reservation is much smaller.
2. *Seminole v. Butterworth,* 657 F.2d 310, U.S. Court of Appeals, Fifth Circuit.

Notes to "Education"

1. *Woodlands: The Story of the Mille Lacs Ojibwe,* oral history video documentary (Onamia, MN: Mille Lacs Band of Ojibwe, 1994); interviews, Melvin Eagle, 2008; James Clark, 2002; Luella Seelye, 2009; David Wallace Adams, *Education for Extinction: American Indians and the Boarding School Experience, 1875–1928* (Lawrence: University Press of Kansas, 1995); Tim Giago, *Children Left Behind: The Dark Legacy of Indian Mission Boarding Schools* (Santa Fe, NM: Clear Light Publishing, 2006); Brenda Child, *Boarding School Seasons: American Indian Families, 1900–1940* (Lincoln: University of Nebraska Press, 1998); James Olson and Raymond Wilson, *Native Americans in the Twentieth Century* (Urbana: University of Illinois Press, 1986); Frederick Hoxie, *The Campaign to Assimilate the Indians* (Lincoln: University of Nebraska Press, 2001); Graves and Ebbott, *Indians in Minnesota,* 16–17, 192–93; Colin Calloway, *First Peoples: A Documentary Survey of American Indian History* (Boston: Bedford/St. Martin's, 2004), 335–96; Janet Chute, *The Legacy of Shingwaukonse: A Century of Native Leadership* (Toronto: University of Toronto Press, 1998).
2. Captain Richard Henry Pratt, as cited on Wikipedia.
3. Commissioner of Indian Affairs William A. Jones, speech to Congress, 1899.
4. The Canadian government issued a formal apology for residential boarding school abuses and a procedure for reparations to those who were abused. The testimonies and reports from that process give us

a clear indication of the patterns and molestation rates in Canada. Information from the U.S. side of the border is more scattered but available in the Merriam Report, other government reports, and numerous articles. See especially Lewis Merriam, *The Problem of Indian Administration: Report of a Survey Made at the Request of Honorable Hubert Work, Secretary of the Interior, and Submitted to Him, February 28, 1928* (Baltimore, MD: Johns Hopkins University Press, 1928), better known as the Merriam Report; and http://archives.cbc.ca/society/education/topics/692.

5. All statistics about the health conditions and death rates at the residential schools are taken from the Merriam Report.

6. Michael Krauss, "Status of Native American Language Endangerment," in ed. Gina Cantoni, *Stabilizing Indigenous Languages* (Flagstaff: Northern Arizona University, 1996), 17.

Notes to "Perspectives"

1. Some studies have proven that it is for many Indians. *Minnesota Statewide Racial Profiling Report;* Williams, "In Minnesota, Claims of Racial Profiling Indians."

2. For Indians living on trust property owned by the tribe, there is an additional obstacle to obtaining loans for housing because the property cannot be mortgaged to a bank, another issue that whites have the privilege of never having to worry about.

Notes to Conclusion

1. Chuck Haga, "A Long Year at Red Lake: From Condemnation to Compassion During a Crisis," *Minneapolis Star Tribune,* Mar. 14, 2006, available at http://www.highbeam.com/doc/1G1-143311115.html.

2. Interview, Thomas Stillday, 2006; Haga, "A Long Year at Red Lake."

3. *Minnesota Statewide Racial Profiling Report;* Williams, "In Minnesota, Claims of Racial Profiling Indians."

4. "Thank you. I'll see you again."

Index

Illustration Credits

Everything You Wanted to Know about Indians But Were Afraid to Ask
was designed and set in type by Judy Gilats in St. Paul, Minnesota.
The typefaces are Alda and Quay Sans.
The book was printed by Worzalla in Stevens Point, Wisconsin.